SELLING
LTCI
TODAY:

46 Ways to Find Clients
and Close More Sales

SELLING

LTCI

TODAY:

46 Ways to Find Clients and Close More Sales

by **Margie Barrie**

Columnist for *Senior Market Advisor*

Author of *50 Ways To Boost Your LTCI Sales*

Selling LTCI Today:
46 Ways to Find Clients and Close More Sales

For information, contact Margie Barrie at: info@margiebarrie.com

ISBN: 978-0-9888919-0-6

Library of Congress Cataloging-in-Publication Data

Category: Long-Term Care Insurance, Sales, Instructional

Book Cover Design and Digital Formatting / Layout by:
Eli Blyden | www.CrunchTimeGraphics.NET

Printed in the United States of America:
A&A Printing | www.printshopcentral.com

Dedication

I am extremely fortunate to be part of four generations of women in one family. As the mother of two sons and grandmother of three boys, I especially value my female family members.

Therefore, I dedicate this book to four important females in my life:

My mother Maxine - She is a great mom, and I'm so appreciative of her unconditional love and support. At age 92, she is still striving to live her life as fully as possible. Her determination to overcome her recent health problems and to resume a normal life is an inspiration.

My two daughters-in-law Danielle and Marianne - I am so proud of their accomplishments. They have achieved the difficult lifestyle balance of having successful careers and being wonderful wives and mothers. I know from personal experience that's not easy.

And to the newest generation, my granddaughter Halsey - Finally, a little girl after two sons and two older grandsons. What a joy in finally having a female to buy for. And, of course, she is so pretty and very brilliant.

Thanks to all of you for being such a special part of my life.

Introduction

By Dr. Marion Somers

TV and Radio Personality, Author and
3in4 Campaign National Spokesperson

As a national spokesperson for the 3in4 Need More Campaign, I have had the opportunity to tour and lecture about long term care (LTC) around the United States. I have been exposed to the care and concerns of individuals, families and businesses regarding the impact of LTC. Having been in the elder care profession for over 40 years, I am aware of the financial and emotional devastation that can occur when people have not prepared for an LTC event. I have met numerous LTC agents during my travels, and I have been extremely impressed with the dedication of these professionals.

People are hungry for information, resources and guidance. We all are comforted when we know what is within our control. When people have the opportunity to ask questions of informed and well-educated LTC agents, many of their anxieties are dissipated. Many of their individual, family and business concerns can be answered with realistic planning. I have always said, *"A failure to plan is a plan to fail."* When people have the opportunity to plan and feel they have all the information they need to make an educated decision, they feel empowered.

That is why I offered to write this introduction, because this book provides such great information to help you, the reader, meet the challenges that are part of being an LTC agent.

I first met Margie Barrie, the national vice president of the 3in4 Association, in the middle of Times Square in 2011, at 7 a.m. on a beautiful May morning. We were both in New York City to officially launch the 3in4 Need More Campaign. The Times Square event was the starting point for the 3in4 national bus tour, where my film crew and I traveled for nine weeks across the country in my antique Greyhound bus.

My second meeting with Margie was a few weeks later when the tour stopped in Baltimore, her hometown. Unfortunately, while Margie was at Times Square, her 90-year-old mother Maxine was rushed to the hospital with double viral pneumonia. Maxine ended up paralyzed in the groin as a result of her antibiotic treatment and had to go to a nursing home for rehabilitation. When the tour stopped in Baltimore, I visited Margie and her mother in the nursing home.

Margie's dedication to her mother was a precious sight. Margie listened to her mother, comforted her, encouraged her, understood her and empathized with her. These same talents, expertise and values have been infused into this book, along with Margie's knowledge, commitment to the LTC industry and dedication to help agents succeed.

You, the reader, get the pleasure of being exposed to her unique perspective, as well as the views of the many writers she has chosen to incorporate into this book. Margie has carefully selected individuals who are powerhouses within the LTC and financial services industries to write the various chapters. Each author shares their unique skill and strength with the reader, thereby giving you the benefit of their combined years of experience for you to integrate and utilize. Each writer is not only helping and guiding you to better understand the individual you are working with and selling to, but also helping you to becoming the best educated agent in your chosen field of specialization within LTC.

A well-informed and educated LTC agent can empower all those who seek answers to their verbalized questions and issues, as well as their yet unspoken questions and issues. No one has a crystal ball to see the future, but being fully informed and educated to the best of one's ability on LTC issues gives us the knowledge and preparation we need.

Each chapter in this book is a separate entity with a unique wealth of information and insight. The book is to be read, enjoyed and absorbed, and will help you be the most resourceful LTC agent for all those who need your help. Be proud of what you do. You are in a unique position to help people.

Little did I think that when I climbed off the bus that day in sunny New York City that two people from such different backgrounds, education and experience would have blended together and be so supportive of each other for a common cause. We have a responsibility to help Americans understand the need for LTC planning and to protect themselves and their families from the perils of an LTC event.

– Marion Somers, Ph.D aka Dr. Marion

Thanks

I have the best of two worlds. First, I love writing about LTC planning; and second, I love working with those who share my dedication to this industry - specifically, the talented people who have worked with me on this book.

First and foremost, Janet Blum has been incredible. Her attention to detail was invaluable in coordinating the numerous details involved in getting the book published and promoting the book through sales and marketing.

Thank you to Ellen Nathan whose talented editing resulted in a manuscript where the copy is of the highest caliber.

Ed Hutman also needs to be recognized for his loyal support and help. For more than 20 years, Ed has been the perfect person for bouncing ideas both off-the-wall and sensible. Both my professional life and my personal life have been made much richer as a result of our long friendship.

I could not have written this book without the support of *Senior Market Advisor* magazine. Twelve years ago I was approached by the then editor to write a monthly article. I turned him down, saying it was too much work. Then – in the middle of the night – I had the idea of doing a column with a question and answer – short, sweet and to the point. I called him the next day and said I would try it and see how it worked. The rest is history. Every time the magazine does a readership survey, my column ranks among the top four. I love writing the column, and I love working with Daniel Williams, the current editor and Maria Wood. They are incredibly supportive and wonderful to work with.

Thank you so much to the talented people who contributed chapter(s) to the book. They are the best! There is something about the LTC insurance industry that causes us to feel that we are not just selling a product. Instead we are on a mission to help people. And it is exciting to me to work with professionals who share that dedication to the cause.

But most of all, thanks to my husband Bernie. He is such a good sport about the many many hours I have been holed up in my (messy) office writing. I could never have completed this manuscript without his loving encourage-ment and support.

A Message From Margie

NOTHING brings home how important
LTC insurance is than having your
OWN MOTHER go on claim!

Those of us in the LTC trenches – with the challenge of selling this protection – we do understand how important this protection is. At conferences and in industry publications, we learn how this coverage helps people and share facts about what happens when an LTC event occurs and coverage is not in place.

And then a claim happens in your immediate family. Stressful? Yes! Frightening? Yes! Overwhelming? Yes!

To briefly summarize the LTC event, my mother, then age 90, was rushed to the hospital with double viral pneumonia. She was treated with an antibiotic that resulted in her becoming paralyzed in the groin. She was then admitted to a rehab facility to learn how to walk again and eventually returned home with around-the-clock home health care. As she improved at home, we were able to cut back the care to seven hours a day. Before her illness, she walked a mile every day; now she is dependent on a walker and sometimes a wheelchair. To complicate the situation, I live 1000 miles away.

So what did I learn from this experience? I realized that these policies offer the following gifts:

- I can supervise the care rather than be forced to provide it hands-on. I don't want to bathe my mother, and she doesn't want me to bathe her either. We now have an aide who does it.

- When my mother went on claim, I didn't have to worry about where to find the money to pay for her care. What assets should I liquidate? Where is her money? Which financial person should I contact? Her stock broker? Her accountant? Instead I just called the carriers' claims departments.

- My mother has two policies – a nursing home policy and a separate home health care policy. Both are with companies no longer writing LTC. Did I have a problem getting the checks? Absolutely not! It was easy, and the follow-up has been excellent.

- My mother lives in Baltimore; I live in Florida. Her policy has enabled me to be a successful long-distance caregiver. When she was in the nursing home, I spent the summer staying at her apartment. But when she came home and things were running smoothly, I could resume my own life. I do go to Baltimore every few months, but I don't need to live there. (And she refuses to move to Florida.)

- Care coordination is wonderful. I thought I knew a lot, but Dr. Marion persuaded me to hire a local care coordinator in my mother's zip code. Thank you Dr. Marion. That was the best advice ever. Harriet Mandel, the person I hired, convinced me to hire a specific home health care agency whose aides were going to nursing school. These aides are bright, caring and, most importantly, my mother loves them.

- My mother worries about money. She has always worried about money and always will. The insurance is paying for about 80 percent of her home health care bill. She is very happy to just pay a small amount from her personal checking account. And right now it means she can easily afford to stay at home and still have sufficient funds to maintain a pleasurable lifestyle.

These policies work! It has provided my mother with the care and support she now needs. And it provides me with peace of mind.

So if you periodically wonder why we agents knock our heads against the wall to convince people to buy this coverage, you now know why I do it.

Contents

PART 4   The Client Presentation

PART 5 Marketing Advice From LTC Experts

PART 1

Getting Referrals From Clients

Chapter 1

How To Get Comfortable Asking For Referrals

By Matt Anderson

Q. *I want to build my practice by getting referrals. How can I get comfortable asking for them?*

There is a basic layer of confidence that needs to be established if you're going to effectively ask for referrals.

1. You only ask for referrals if you've earned them - Too much of what we hear about referrals is based around techniques: how to ask, when to ask, what to say and who to get them from. We don't spend enough time focusing on what we are actually doing to earn the word-of-mouth recommendation. Neither you nor your clients recommend someone unless they deserve it, unless in the other person's eyes, something truly valuable has been delivered. Expectations must be exceeded. If you have only done your job, you cannot expect someone to tell others.

Part of your referral conversation should include a discussion about what your client has gotten out of working with you. This will tell you whether you should be asking. This is the first layer. If you have brought value, this makes asking much easier.

2. Understand why people refer you - Andy Sernovitz's research at Northwestern University has found that there are two main reasons why people refer others. First, referring you to other people in their life makes *them* feel good. Second, they like to help people *they* care about. Notice neither of these reasons has anything to do with you. It's not about you; it's about them.

They are motivated about what's important to *them*. Knowing this can build your confidence because now you don't have to fear looking needy – their world does not revolve around you! It revolves around people who *they* would like to help – who are also hopefully good prospects for you.

The second layer then in building your confidence is making sure your referral request focuses on how your happy client might be able to help others. It's not a conversation about how you grow your business because most of the time other people do not care about this.

3. Have empowering beliefs about asking for referrals - When it comes to asking for referrals, most people believe that they are being pushy by asking or that it makes them look needy if they are asking. You must ask yourself what concerns you have about asking.

Your beliefs create your reality. Unfortunately, 87 percent of the thoughts we have are unconscious ones – habitual thoughts that are mostly negative and unhelpful. The solution is to change your beliefs by coming up with one that empowers you to ask. Provided your client recognizes that you have brought value and you ask in a way that's about your client helping others, fears you have about looking pushy or cheesy are completely unfounded.

The biggest difference between people who get many referrals and those who don't is that the successful ones think differently. They have mostly empowering beliefs about asking for referrals that encourage them toward what they want. The most empowering belief you can have about getting referrals is this: I'm good at what I do. I can help people you care about and I know I need to ask you!

One exercise I recommend is to list 20 reasons why someone should do business with you. You have to become your number one fan. For some advisors, this is where the light bulb goes on and a third layer of confidence is built. Simply putting in some time thinking hard about the value that you bring to the table can make a significant difference. It compares to when you first started in the business and were unsure at times about what you were saying, hoping nobody would ask you a question you didn't know the answer to. Think back to that time and remember also that at some later date you were in a meeting and consciously realized that all those doubts were gone because you did know your stuff! You were making eye contact with assurance. That's the kind of transition you can experience with asking for referrals as well.

Warning: Be ready for your brain to resist change. Your unhelpful beliefs are not going to be substituted without a fight. Amazingly, our habitual thoughts are 1,000 times stronger than a new one. Even when your status quo is unhelpful, your brain will still fight to keep you in this so-called comfort zone.

4. Pre-plan your asks - A fourth layer of confidence will be there if you go into a meeting knowing what your referral request is. What door would you like opened by your happy client? This is an incredibly important habit to develop. Then you don't spend time distracted during the meeting wondering who to ask for.

If your initial response to this idea is "I often don't know who they know," then you first need to develop the habit of what I call "fishing." Fish during your time with that client for important people in their life who they like. Who do they know that might make a good prospect for you? You can't expect them to figure this out on the spot, so your conversation should include this activity.

5. Know when the best time is to ask for referrals - The best time to ask is when your client is most happy with your work. Clearly that is when he or she will go to bat for you most enthusiastically. The only thing that complicates this topic is your self-doubt. Again, if your client recognizes that you have brought value, it is okay to ask.

An even better time is after such a meeting when you have stopped talking business and are just chatting about something light, pleasant and more personal. People relax at this time, and it feels more natural and less formal to bring up a referral request as an after-thought. This works well and psychologically feels right too.

—

Matt Anderson
The Referral Authority
Phone: 312-622-3121
Email: matt@thereferralauthority.com
Website: www.thereferralauthority.com
International author and speaker, Matt helps business people expand their marketing territory by mastering the art of business referrals. Matt is the author of *Fearless Referrals™ – How to Ask in a Way That's Comfortable for YOU and Market Yourself For Free.*

Chapter 2

Putting Referrals On Your Agenda

By Richard Harris, Ph.D.

Q. *I need to increase referrals. Can you suggest a system where I can accomplish that and feel more comfortable asking clients who they know?*

Referrals are recognized as the best source for acquiring new quality clients. To get the referrals that are waiting for you, control is essential to implement the referral process consistently and effectively and to overcome the uncomfortable feelings that will inhibit you from making it happen.

Two factors can sabotage the entire referral effort. First is the high energy focus on making the sale, which should be the professional's top priority as it's the basis for getting paid. The downside is that it can distract you from the referral process.

The second factor is that the referral process can be uncomfortable for both you and your referral source. If those uncomfortable feelings are not controlled, they can severely hamper referral productivity.

Here are some of the more common referral discomforts:

- I just closed the sale; I don't want to do anything to jeopardize this accomplishment by pushing for referrals.

- I don't want my prospect/client to think I'm just a pushy salesman by asking for referrals.

- I don't want my friend to be upset that I gave his name to an insurance agent.

- I don't know if they have a need for my services.

Your agenda

Your tool for staying in control of the referral is your prepared agenda. This will be used as a road map listing topics to be discussed and objectives to be attained.

Numerous benefits can be derived from using this tool. You will:

1. Control meetings with prospects and clients much more effectively.

2. Be perceived by others as being highly professional.

3. Reduce consumer wariness of your intentions.

4. Create feelings of respect, inclusion and trust – these are essential for client acquisition and development.

5. Help people make decisions and avoid procrastination.

6. Earn the source's recommendation, which will be the basis for securing referrals.

Here is a sample agenda:

Prepared For the Approval of (Name)

- Introduction - I would like to give you information about myself and the firm with which I am associated.

- Taking care of your needs and wants - I would like to show you the process that I use for being of service to my clients

- Solutions

- Decisions - I will help you make a decision which is in your best interests.

- Earning your recommendation - I would like you to feel so comfortable with my services that I will earn your recommendation to people you know.

The last item on our agenda has been left open. Is there any information you need or questions you have that we should be talking about?

Presenting the agenda for approval

After the initial rapport-building conversation, you present the agenda for approval with the following statement: *"In preparation for our discussion today, I've put together an agenda of the topics I thought would be important for us to cover. I'd like to present it to you and see if it meets with your approval."*

After completing the first two items of the agenda, you are now ready to implement the recommendation item. To do so, begin by securing feedback: *"How do you feel about the process we have just gone through? How do you feel about our work together so far?"*

Once feedback has been received, then say, *"The last item on our agenda is recommendations. Would you feel comfortable proceeding with recommendations today, or would you prefer to wait until our next contact* (if a second appointment has been set)*?"*

The next step is to make arrangements for you to be introduced to the referral. This introduction needs to incorporate the recommendations of your source, since it is their prestige or influence with the lead that is the key for future business possibilities. The most typical strategy uses a testimonial note, a letter from you and then a telephone call.

Following is an example of a letter to use:

Heading
Dear (Name),

Your name was mentioned by (referrer) in a meeting we recently had. (Referrer) has not had a reason to believe that you were seeking financial services, but did think that our meeting might be of benefit to you . . .if not for a current financial need, then perhaps for one in the future.

I will call in a few days to introduce myself and arrange a time for us to meet.

In the meantime, if you would like to contact (referrer) regarding my services, please feel free to do so.

Best regards,
(Your Name)

What if the client counters your request for recommendations with a concern? Here are some frequent client concerns and ways to address them.

- **Let me think about it** – *"That's fine. Would you mind sharing with me the things you would like to think about?"*

- **I can't think of anybody** - *"I understand. That's common. In anticipation of this, I have taken the time to prepare a list of people who I believe you might know"* or *"You had mentioned that you have a brother and sister who live nearby. Could you tell me about them? Work, family, etc."*

- **Let me call them first** - *"We could do that, although I often find that people get so busy it's easy to lose track of the calls. Perhaps we can first send an Introducing Card and letter that I showed you. Then you can call and, as I indicate in my letter, I will also call them to request an appointment. By the way, when you do call, please*

> *mention the basis for my contact is not to sell them anything, but to explore their possible need, now or in the future, for my services. Is this procedure acceptable to you"*

- **I would like to wait** - "*We do have another appointment scheduled next week. It sounds as if you would like to wait until then to consider offering your recommendations. That's fine.*"

- **I don't believe in giving referrals** - "*I understand. Many people feel that way. May I ask why you reached that decision? I hope in time, after we have had a chance to work together, you would feel that I would not create any problems for you as others have. Can you keep an open mind to this possibility?*"

- **I'm not comfortable at this time** - "*I understand. May I ask what is making you uncomfortable at this point*"

- **You haven't earned my recommendation yet** - "*May I ask what things I need to work on so that I can have an opportunity to earn your recommendations sometime in the future?*"

Telephone techniques

Here is a script to use when calling the referral.

"*Hello, (First name of lead), this is (your name and organization). In a meeting that I recently had with (source), he/she mentioned your name." (Make a personal comment.)*

"(First name of source) nor I had any reason to believe that you were currently in the market for a financial product, but we did feel that it may be helpful for us to meet and discuss some areas which you might find beneficial. Would next Tuesday afternoon be convenient to meet or would you prefer another time?"

Following are some objections you might encounter and how to handle them.

- **No need -** *"I understand, but for now I would just like an opportunity to get acquainted - if not for an immediate need, then perhaps for one which might arise in the future. May I ask what your financial priorities are at this present time?"*

- **No money -** *"I understand, but if you do have a need, I feel it's my responsibility to help you find a way to take care of it within your budget. May I ask what your financial priorities are at the present time?"*

- **Has an advisor -** *"I understand, but having a second opinion when making an important financial decision just might save you some money. May I ask what your financial priorities are at the present time?"*

- **Timing not right -** *"I understand that you have other priorities right now, but I would just like an opportunity to get acquainted. May I ask what your financial priorities are at the present time?*

- **For those resisting any future discussion -** *"One's circumstances have a way of changing over time. May I call you at a later time? (If the reply is yes, focus upon a potential need.) In preparing for that call, if you were to identify an area that had a priority for you - such as maximizing investments, retirement planning, CD alternatives, college education funding, etc. - what would it be?"*

After the need has been identified, indicate that some information relevant to that need will be mailed. Include a handwritten note along with the mailing to make the contact more personalized. Schedule a follow-up telephone call at an agreed-upon time.

You now have the system for taking control of referrals. That means that instead of asking for referrals, you will be expecting them.

Richard Harris, Ph.D.

Phone: 941-284-3462
Email: expectrecommendations@gmail.com
Website: www.referralvalues.com
Richard's program, *The Formula For Doubling Your Production*, teaches financial advisors how to use a referral system instead of cold calling in their prospecting and marketing efforts.

Chapter 3

A Step-By-Step Process To Get Referrals

By Sid Walker

Q. *Can you provide me with a practical step-by-step process of how to ask for a referral?*

There are a number of important steps to successfully get the referral. I have divided the process into four parts.

1. How to ask for help from the referral source

- When asking for help, give 'em a way out.

  "John, I would like to ask for your help but with one condition, (Pause.) I don't want your help unless you are comfortable doing so. Does that sound fair?"

- Sell them on the benefits of helping you.

  "I would like to talk to you about getting some introductions to people you know. Let me tell you how I would like to do this. The main reason an introduction works so well is that when I call

someone and I say I know you, most people will give me 10 to 15 minutes of their time, out of courtesy to you. So I get a chance to meet most people."

"This is a very social process. It really isn't a sales call. You could call it networking, because the worst that can happen when I am introduced to someone is that we become a resource for each other for the future. And, I'm not looking for someone who's in the market to buy anything. I just want to meet people. However, I am looking for people who are doing well financially."

- Explain what you will do.

"I like to make the introduction process as easy as possible for everyone involved. What I do is send out this letter with your name at the bottom in bold (Show client a sample letter). *Frankly, what the letter says isn't as important as having your name at the bottom. With your name on this letter, I will get to see most people for a few minutes. And that is all I want, just a few minutes to introduce myself and say hello. The rest of the conversation is up to the prospect."*

If I would like to send a letter to a referral, I close the conversation by saying, *"So my question is, John, would you be comfortable having me send this letter to people you know?"* If I do not plan to send a letter, I close with, *"So*

*my question is, John, would you be comfortable introducing
me to people you know on this basis?"*

2. What to send and how

I like letters with people's names at the bottom in the
postscript. Hundreds of my clients say that this approach
works extremely well, and they agree that it's one of the
easiest approaches for all concerned.

Regardless if you are writing a note or a letter to a referral,
it is important to talk benefits. Make a list of all the benefits
of your product or service. Then pick the top one or two
benefits and make sure you talk about these benefits in the
letter. Too often, salespeople speak in terms of features,
without giving enough information about benefits. A good
test to determine whether or not you have a strong enough
benefit information is to ask, *"What's the benefit in the
long run?"* after each statement describing what you do for
people. For example, *"We help people make educated
decisions that feel right to them."* What is the long-range
benefit? (Example: peace of mind.) It may be implied, but
not stated clearly. Two sample letters and a telephone script
appear in the next chapter.

3. How to work with a referral

When I meet with a referral, I follow this sales process:

- Start with small talk.

- Give a general statement of benefits by describing
  my work.

- Give a purpose for the meeting and what to expect.

  "I teach people how to avoid the most common mistakes in the _____ area. Most of the people I talk to feel their time with me was time well spent."

- Obtain permission to ask questions.

  "Jim, so I can make sure I am talking about things that are of interest to you, could I ask you a few questions?"

- Begin by asking easy questions that are directly or indirectly related to your product or service, including questions relating to what his/her experience has been with your product or service.

  "What has he/she done? Why? Likes or dislikes? Has anyone in your family required at-home care? Are the parents still living? etc."

- Explain the three things people like most about your product or service. Then ask which one would be most important to him/her, and why.

- Show a list of benefits related to the problems your products/services address.

- Determine which of your products/services might be of interest to the referral and why.

- Show how your products/services would benefit the referral.

4. Very important additional things to do

- Make the referral source look forward to having you call their friends.

  Ask, *"What do they like about them?"* or *"What is outstanding about this guy?"* Then ask, *"Would it be okay if I told him you said that?"*

- Obtain permission to check back with the individual for additional names. This is worth a fortune!

  "Can I call you in a few months to see who you've met?" or *"Can I call you from time to time to see if you have met anyone interesting?"*

- If your referral language is not working, or you are just not asking, winging it is probably not your best bet at this stage. Try to learn the language the way it is written to start out. Try not to change the content or the flow. This language is highly tested with hundreds of advisors.

Of course, if something doesn't feel right to you, then don't use it. My biggest challenge is to get people to memorize this language and try it few times so they can see it work. Then, you can make all the modifications you want! Once you see this language works, most advisors don't change it much.

Remember that your goal is to find the people who are comfortable promoting you. This is not about trying to wrestle referrals out of your clients. If they say they want to think about it or get back to you, make a note in your file and bring it up again when you see them again. What they may be saying is that they are not comfortable with the referral process no matter how much they like you. That's fine. You don't need everyone to give you referrals to be extremely successful at this process!

Sidney C. Walker

Sales Performance Coach for Relationship-Oriented Financial Advisors
Phone: 877-985-3297
Email: Sid@SidWalker.com
Website: www.SidWalker.com
Website: www.sellingwithoutwrestling.com
Sid is the founder of the *Selling Without Wrestling Society* and the author of six books on topics including: interviewing to get more client commitment, how to develop the confidence to prospect for bigger clients, overcoming call reluctance and the fear of self-promotion, and how to "get on a roll" and "stay on a roll" selling financial services.

Chapter 4

Referral Letters That Work!

By Sid Walker

Q. *Could you please provide samples of the letters that Sid recommends for sending to referral sources and to the person to whom you are referred?*

The following letter includes many of the ideas that I have presented thus far. Please realize that these materials are primarily targeted for financial planners, but can easily be adapted for the long term care sale.

Sample letter for the referral source

Heading
Dear _____:

I'm writing this letter to ask for your help, but with one condition. The condition is that I only want your help if you are comfortable doing so. I have found that my best source of new business comes from being introduced to people by my friends and clients. I am not looking for people who are in the market to buy anything at this time. I am simply looking for people who appreciate hearing about constructive ways to get the most out of the money they earn.

I like to make the introduction process as easy as possible for everyone involved. What I do is send out the enclosed letter with your name in bold at the bottom. Frankly, what the letter says isn't as important as having your name on it. With your name at the bottom, I will get to meet over 95 percent of the people I call. Without a name, the percentage goes down considerably. So you can see that being introduced in this way makes a huge difference in my effectiveness and time management.

When I meet people for the first time, I like to keep the meeting short. I mainly want to have a chance to introduce myself and get to know each other for a few minutes. If they find something interesting in what I have to say and want to meet with me again, that's up to them. Either way, I like to be a resource to the people I meet, knowing that some of them will become clients in the future.

Would you be willing to allow me to send my letter to some people you know? In most cases, people won't bother to call you to ask about me. They will simply give me a few minutes out of courtesy to you and leave it at that. If someone does call you to ask about me, I am mainly asking for a character reference. Just tell them I am a good person worth talking to for a few minutes. I will call you in a few days to find out if you would be comfortable introducing me on this basis.

Sincerely,

Sample letters to the referred person

Sample letter 1 - I have found this letter to be extremely effective both for me and for hundreds of my financial services clients.

Heading
Dear _____:

Within the next few days, I will be contacting you to ask your permission to meet with you at your convenience. I have no reason to believe you are presently interested in equity investments or insurance planning, but you have been described to me as a person who is interested in constructive ideas.

My ideas involve ways to maximize your before-tax income. I assure you that I will be brief and that subsequent meetings will be arranged at your request. I will not attempt to sell you any products during this interview. I simply want to meet you and share some information that has been very valuable to many people like yourself. I hope that we can get together on this basis.

Sincerely,
P.S. Prior to my calling, you may want to refer to (name of source) regarding me and the type of service I offer.

Sample letter 2 - This letter has a little different format. The referral's name is mentioned twice in the body of the letter instead of in the postscript.

Heading

Dear _____:

I recently had the pleasure of meeting and doing some work for (name of source). In the process of our conversation, your name was mentioned as a leader in your field who is open to new and constructive ideas.

My service is designed to _____ (list benefits here). I promise to be brief and that subsequent meetings will be at your request. I will give you a call within a week to arrange a convenient time to meet you and introduce myself. In the interim, if you have any questions about me or my services, please don't hesitate to give (first name of referrer) a call.

Kind regards,

What to say on the telephone

Some people don't want to take the time or trouble to send a letter. They like to get on the telephone and call. Sending a letter first doesn't necessarily work better than simply calling people with no introduction. You have to discover what approach works best for you.

Calling a referral on the telephone is like any other kind of telephone sales call. You want to be upbeat and sound like someone who is enjoying life, someone who would be interesting to meet. What you say is secondary to how you feel when you say it. If you are feeling relaxed and confident with a genuine desire to meet new people, this will come through in your voice. If you can, give people a reputation to live up to by telling them the good things their referrer said about them. If you don't want to quote the referrer, make a general complimentary statement about him/her.

Keep it simple. Talk in terms of the general benefits of your product or service. Don't get into too much detail over the telephone. Your main objective is to get an appointment with people who are open to having one or showing some interest.

The most significant difference when calling a referral is that you have a name you can use; and you want to mention the referrer's name right away.

Your language could be something like this:

Sample language 1

You: *"Jim, this is Sid Walker. We have not met, but I was talking with John Garrison recently, and he had some very complimentary things to say about you."* [Pause]

Jim: *"Oh, is that right?"*

You*: "Yes, as a matter of fact, he said you were a very sharp businessman and that you and I should have a chance to meet.*

And that's why I'm calling. I wanted to see if we could get together for a few minutes so I can introduce myself in person and tell you a little bit about the work I do to help people maximize what they are doing with their money. Can you squeeze me in next week for a few minutes?"

Sample language 2

You: *"Tim, this is Sid Walker. Do you have a minute to talk?"*

Tim: *"I've just got a couple of minutes before I have to go out."*

You: *"That's fine. I will keep it short. I was talking to our mutual friend, Larry Johnson, the other day, and he had some very good things to say about you."*

Tim: (Pauses, doesn't say anything.)

You: *"You know Larry, don't you?"*

Tim: *"Oh, sure, I know him. Larry is a good friend."*

You: *"Well, Larry thought that you and I would enjoy meeting and that's why I'm calling. I specialize in helping people maximize what they are doing with their money, and I wanted to stop by briefly and introduce myself."*

Sample language 3

You: *"I was talking to a friend of yours recently, Cathy Hubbard."*

Kay: *"Oh, sure. I know Cathy."*

You: *"Cathy had some very complimentary things to say about you, and one of those things was that you are open to new ideas on how maximize what you are doing with your money. That's also the reason for my call. I was wondering if we might be able to get together for a few minutes next week so I can formally introduce myself."*

Kay: *"What do you do?"*

You: *"I help people maximize what they are doing with their money. I am not calling with the idea that you are in the market for anything in particular. Cathy felt you and I would enjoy meeting each other, and I was hoping you might have a few minutes next week. Can you squeeze me in?"*

Remember, your objective is to get an appointment with someone showing interest or a willingness to meet. If your referred prospect is clearly not interested and you sense a meeting would be a waste of time, move on to the next prospect. Most people are naturally a little cautious about talking to someone they don't know. However, you can sense if you are getting a weak excuse that just needs some additional encouragement on your part or if your referred prospect is truly not interested.

Sidney C. Walker

Sales Performance Coach for Relationship-Oriented Financial Advisors
Phone: 877-985-3297
Email: Sid@SidWalker.com
Website: www.SidWalker.com
Website: www.sellingwithoutwrestling.com

Sid is the founder of the *Selling Without Wrestling Society* and the author of six books on topics including: interviewing to get more client commitment, how to develop the confidence to prospect for bigger clients, overcoming call reluctance and the fear of self-promotion, and how to "get on a roll" and "stay on a roll" selling financial services.

Chapter 5

Pursuing Higher Quality Leads: Who's Hot & Who's Not

By Sid Walker

Q. I want to pursue higher quality referrals. How do I determine who would be a hot referral and who would not?

The term "Power Referral" describes a referral that comes from someone who has a substantial influence with the person he/she is referring. A New York Life study concluded that when the referrer had significant influence with the person he/she was referring, it was twice as effective as a referral from a social acquaintance. Twice as effective, in this case, meant that twice as many people bought something.

Being asked to give introductions to your friends can easily become very psychologically complex. There has been a lot of study and documentation of what is called

31

social styles. These are general behavior preferences that can be readily observed.

Two basic continuums determine social style. One continuum has assertive on one side and more cautious on the other. The other continuum has thinking on one side and feeling on the other. When you lay these two continuums one on top of the other to form four right-angle quadrants, it creates four basic social styles. The four groups are: assertive thinkers, assertive feelers, more cautious thinkers and more cautious feelers.

	Thinkers	Feelers
Assertive	Assertive thinkers	Assertive feelers
More cautious	More cautious thinkers	More cautious feelers

Generally speaking, the assertive feelers and thinkers are going to be more comfortable giving you referrals. They like to have influence over other people, and they like to test that influence. On the other hand, the more cautious thinkers and feelers are not as interested in testing their influence. They want to get along and be liked at all costs, and are much less likely to want to risk any potential conflicts by making introductions or giving referrals.

When you look at the makeup of the population, roughly speaking, the assertive thinkers make up about 20 percent of the population and the assertive feelers about 10 percent.

So about 30 percent of the population is generally open to giving referrals, if they like you and what you're doing. The more cautious feelers are the largest group at 50 percent, and the more cautious thinkers are 20 percent. Therefore, about 70 percent of the population is not very excited about making introductions.

There is an additional positive factor in favor of getting referrals. As human beings, we are much more complicated than any four-quadrant profile can predict. In fact, most social style profiles break the four main quadrants down into 16 additional identifiable profiles. What this means is that there is a large group of the more cautious thinkers and more cautious feelers who have a backup social style that is more assertive. My guess is that about one-third to one-half of the more cautious group has a backup style that is assertive; and they are therefore; generally open to giving referrals under the right conditions.

What does all this mean in terms of who is comfortable giving referrals? Generally speaking, in terms of social styles, I predict that approximately 50 percent of any mixed group of people is going to be comfortable giving referrals if they like you and what you are offering. This, of course, means that the other 50 percent of the group is not going to be comfortable introducing you to anyone. So if you're expecting that everyone will give you referrals, you're going to be disappointed. The reality is that there's a large group of people who are never going to be comfortable giving you referrals, no matter what you do. If half of the people you establish some kind of relationship with give you referrals, you're at the head of the class.

When is the best time to ask?

When is the best time to ask for referrals? The conventional wisdom says ask whenever the prospect or client is feeling good about you, the work you're doing or the work you've done. This is often at the time of delivery of the product or service, if the sales process requires several calls. If you're in a one-call close situation, the time to ask is when people have made a positive decision or have demonstrated in some way that they like you, your product or your service.

There are a number of ways to contact your referrals once you have successfully acquired their names. Any of the following have worked well for many agents. You have to decide what works best for you.

- Send a note or letter on your letterhead, on stationery or on something that is personalized.

- Ask the referrer to write the note or letter.

- Send the referral a note or letter from you with a note from your referrer on it, or with the referrer's name at the bottom in bold in the postscript.

- Send the referral a letter with your hand-written postscript at the bottom with the referrer's name in it.

- Send a letter mentioning the referrer in bold face in the body of the letter.

- Call your referral on the telephone.

- Have your referrer call the referrals while you're in his or her office.

—

Sidney C. Walker

Sales Performance Coach for Relationship-Oriented Financial Advisors

Phone: 877-985-3297

Email: Sid@SidWalker.com

Website: www.SidWalker.com

Website: www.sellingwithoutwrestling.com

Sid is the founder of the *Selling Without Wrestling Society* and the author of six books on topics including: interviewing to get more client commitment, how to develop the confidence to prospect for bigger clients, overcoming call reluctance and the fear of self-promotion, and how to "get on a roll" and "stay on a roll" selling financial services.

Chapter 6

The Prospecting Mentality: How To Overcome Call Reluctance, Procrastination And Sleepless Nights

By Sid Walker

Q. *How do I know if I have what it takes to be an effective prospector?*

Effective prospecting skills are essential for an agent to be successful. Here are the characteristics of an effective prospecting mentality:

- Have an ability to continually monitor the bigger picture. They are not overly concerned with any one aspect, circumstance or event along the path to achieving their goal. They view seeking out new business as an ever-changing flow of events rather than a predictable technical procedure. They know and accept the reality that there is always an unknown element when working with people.

- Have a tireless ability to maintain a positive vision no matter what happens and keep their eye on their long-term goals. Furthermore, with a positive vision and goals that feel intuitively right, they know their vision will somehow become a reality.

- Trust their ability to succeed and are not concerned with how they succeed, as long as it is done with integrity.

- Trust the power of their intuitive instincts to creatively guide them along the most effective and efficient path to achieving their goals.

- Possess no fear of making mistakes, since they see their mistakes as a required part of the process of reaching their goals.

- Have no fear of failure because they view failure merely as a negative judgment about how things have turned out thus far. Their perspective says the only way to fail is to quit before it feels intuitively right to do so.

- Do not need to know how things will turn out before taking action. They simply trust that if they do what feels right with a positive vision, they will succeed in one of two ways: 1) They will either get the result they want, or 2) They will learn something that is required to achieve the result. In this way, they know in their heart and soul, they really can't lose.

- Have fun meeting and getting to know new people. They enjoy being warm, friendly and spontaneous with people. They have a sense of humor and sensitivity to what others are feeling.

- Give each call 100 percent of their creativity, skill and sensitivity. They treat each call as if it were a totally new experience, being ready to sense the subtle differences in people.

- Do not care who buys and who doesn't. They are looking for the right people to work with, based on the right chemistry and timing, rather than trying to force a relationship with people who don't really want one.

Checklist for a prospecting mentality

If you meet the criteria listed above, here is a list of what you need to pledge to do when prospecting:

- I accept the reality of prospecting and realize that no matter how skilled I am or how wonderful my products are, some people are going to be interested and some are not.

- I accept that I don't know which of the people I call on are going to be interested; and I accept the certainty that if I continue to make calls, there will be people who are interested in what I am offering.

It's like rolling dice. It's guaranteed that some rolls are going to be winners. I never know for sure which ones are going to be winners until after I have rolled the dice.

- I accept that there are plenty of people for me to work with. And if someone isn't interested in what I'm offering, it may simply be that the timing isn't right for us to have a business relationship.

- I accept the Chemistry and Timing Formula that says I am going to hit it off with some of the people I meet and that some of those people are going to be ready for what I'm offering. For the most part, the elements of chemistry and timing are out of my control, so I shouldn't get overly involved in trying to make things happen that don't seem to want to happen.

- I accept the reality that it is my responsibility to regularly initiate prospecting activity. It's as much a part of life as it's a part of my job to regularly seek out people who are interested in what I have to offer. I accept the unknown elements of prospecting and realize it's an ever-changing art rather than a predictable science. The only way I'm going to know who might be interested is to make the call.

- I accept that the only way I can lose at prospecting is not to do it. I have everything to gain with the smallest of efforts in the right direction. The key is to maintain a momentum by regularly asking people if they might have an interest in what I'm offering.

Sidney C. Walker

Sales Performance Coach for Relationship-Oriented Financial Advisors
Phone: 877-985-3297
Email: Sid@SidWalker.com
Website: www.SidWalker.com
Website: www.sellingwithoutwrestling.com
Sid is the founder of the *Selling Without Wrestling Society* and the author of six books on topics including: interviewing to get more client commitment, how to develop the confidence to prospect for bigger clients, overcoming call reluctance and the fear of self-promotion, and how to "get on a roll" and "stay on a roll" selling financial services.

Chapter 7

Seven Ways To Get Referrals Without Asking

By Bill Cates

Q. *How can I convince my clients to give me referrals?*

Here are seven proven ways to promote providing referrals to your clients, along with sample scripts. About 70% of the time, these techniques will result in your clients giving you referrals at some time in the future. However, you can expect that about 30% of the time, these techniques will generate referrals right on the spot.

1. Reminder of confidentiality - Some clients are reluctant to give referrals because they fear information about their financial situation may be shared with others. Here's a way you can plant a seed for referrals and handle a major objection at the same time.

"George, there's one thing I want to run by you. Many of my clients like to introduce me to those who they think would benefit from my services. I just wanted you to know

that, should that opportunity present itself, the work we do here is always kept confidential. I will never tell them about your financial situation, and vice versa."

2. Who you serve best - One reason why you may not always get the type of referrals you want is because your clients aren't clear as to whom you serve. First, become crystal clear yourself. Then communicate your client profile to your clients in a low-key way that plants a nice seed for referrals.

"I thought it would be good for you to know who would benefit most from my services. These days, my practice is geared toward individuals or couples between the ages of 45 and 75. They usually have children, but not always. While I don't expect you to know their financial situation or even if they'd be interested in the important work I do, if you care about them, I think you'd agree that they should at least know about me. Make sense?" [Note: Insert your ideal client profile into this template.]

3. How I'll contact them - A major concern clients have is how you will handle any referrals they may provide to you. You can alleviate their concern and plant a seed at the same time. Later, when you ask them directly for referrals, they will already know how you intend to handle them.

"I don't like to surprise people with a phone call out of the blue. I've found that everyone feels most comfortable when they know I'll be contacting them and have a sense of why I'm doing so. If you identify someone you think should know

about the important work that I do, please come to me first. Together, we'll figure out the best way to approach these folks. We'll do it in a way that suits your relationship with them and that feels comfortable and natural to everyone involved. If they are interested, great, we'll meet for a no-obligation review – such as I did initially with you. If they decide that they don't want to move forward, I assure you I won't pressure or pester them. How does that sound?

4. Don't keep me a secret - Many financial professionals are using this phrase with great success. It often results in a referral conversation right on the spot. Try saying this to your clients at the end of a meeting. Add it as a PS to your handwritten notes. You can even add it to your email signature file and your voice mail.

5. Willingness to give referrals - This is a great technique to get a referral conversation with anyone who is a small business owner, salesperson, or anyone who needs referrals for their business. You can use it with your prospects, clients, friends, people you meet at social functions, or even neighbors you meet at your kids' soccer games.

"Frank, you sound like you do pretty good work for your clients. Tell me, if I ran into a good prospect for your business, how would I know it and how would you like me to introduce you to them?"

When you demonstrate a genuine willingness to give referrals, many people will reciprocate with you. This can be a great start to a productive Center of Influence relationship.

6. Celebrate referrals - Every time you meet a new prospect through a referral, make a big deal about it. Talk about the person you know in common.

"It's great Tom introduced me to you. When I meet folks through referrals like this, it leaves me with more time to serve my clients, instead of spending time looking for clients. Make sense? And, quite frankly, it's how most people prefer to meet their financial professionals, such as myself."

7. Who should I thank - I suggest you put the following message on your voice mail. This sends the message to all who call you that you get referrals on a regular basis – you are referable. And that you have an attitude of gratitude.

"This is Mike Smith. Sorry I missed your call. Please leave a message at the tone. And if you were referred to us, please let us know who we need to thank."

Bill Cates, CSP

Founder, The Referral Coach
Email: info@referralcoach.com
Website: www.referralminute.com
Bill is the author of *Get More Referrals Now!* and *Don't Keep Me a Secret!* His books, speeches and video-training programs have revolutionized the way financial professionals acquire more and better clients through referrals.

Chapter 8

Delivering The Policy = Referrals

By Aaron Eisenach

Q. *I need help developing referral sources, particularly with attorneys, accountants and other insurance agents who do not sell LTCI or are uncomfortable doing so. How do you suggest I accomplish this?*

Getting referrals and developing centers of influence, such as lawyers and CPA's, are two of the best ways to generate quality leads. I say this from personal experience. More significantly, the success of this approach has been documented by LIMRA when it studied sources of sales.

I have developed a very effective and easy system for building a referral base by asking for the names of advisors when delivering a LTCI policy to a client. Here's what I teach my agents to do: After collecting the appropriate signatures and any remaining premium balance during policy delivery, have a sheet of paper ready to take down the names of the advisors with whom the client is already working. You may want to develop your own form with blanks for the names and phone numbers so the client sees that you need these names.

Here are sample scripts that you may choose to adopt:

- *"Mr. Client, it's very important that your team of advisors know about this protection you have put in place. With your permission, I will gladly take care of this for you."*

- *"Should something ever happen to you, it may be your kids who are trying to find this policy and someone to call for help. In case they call your home and auto insurance agent, I want to make sure your agent has my card and a copy of your Policy Schedule Page. Who is your agent?"*

- *"You may be able to benefit from some tax savings by purchasing this policy. I get many questions from tax professionals who do not know what to do with LTCI premiums. Who is your CPA or accountant?"*

- *"Your financial advisor needs to know that you have taken care of this piece of your retirement and estate plan. He/she will want to mark it off the list of things to do. Who is your financial advisor?"*

- *"Do you have a family attorney? Is there someone who has prepared your will or trust or advance medical directives? I need to let him/her know about this as well."*

Other strategies

Here are some other strategies that have worked well for me:

- To prepare clients for this request, when you are taking the application mention that you will be asking for these names upon policy delivery. Emphasize that this is a decision that needs to be made known to others, not kept secret.

- Don't ask for these names during the application meeting. You run the risk of reminding clients that their financial advisor or property and casualty agent may offer the same coverage.

- You may not want to take the time to collect phone numbers of the advisors. The advisor's name and his/her company will suffice if you're pressed for time. Then simply find their contact information online.

- When telephoning the advisors, make it short and sweet, and do not give away too much information. Try something like this: "*Mr./Ms. P&C agent, I specialize in long term care insurance, and we have a client in common. I would like to come by your office and share with you the client's Policy Schedule Page and give you my card for your client's file in case you are ever contacted by the family. Can I borrow ten minutes of your time on Thursday at 10 a.m.?*"

- Don't give them the name of the client or discuss the carrier or policy details over the phone. They have to meet you to get this information.

- Chances are, the advisor does not own LTCI; and you should plan on stretching the ten minutes you have asked for into longer, but only if it's convenient to the advisor.

- Be aware that the advisor may offer LTCI and is not happy that his/her client went elsewhere. An offer to split commissions (provided he/she is properly licensed) may prevent harming the relationship between the advisor and the client and may lead to referrals from the advisor. The advisor likely doesn't write much LTCI and would benefit from partnering with a trustworthy professional.

- Be ready to speak with the advisor about ways to reach his/her client base. Many carriers make available attractive direct mail pieces and other marketing materials. You may also discuss educational workshops featuring you as the expert.

- Financial advisors and licensed insurance agents may be rightly concerned about future liability if a suitable LTCI plan has not been put in place. Recommend, and perhaps offer, a form that requires a signature from the client that LTCI has been offered and declined.

- Always be polite and professional. Pay attention to your appearance.

- Have a stack of business cards with you when visiting the advisors. Learn to expect referrals.

By using this method for every policy you sell, you will potentially have the names of three or four people who may provide you with referrals or become your clients themselves!

Aaron Eisenach, CLTC
Regional Vice President, Individual Commercial Brokerage Inc. (ICB), Denver, CO
Phone: 800-788-8205
Email: aaron.e@ica-icb.com
Website: www.ica-icb.com
As a national LTC brokerage, we assist producers with selling and marketing traditional and linked LTC solutions. I also teach Colorado's mandated LTC classroom courses.

PART 2

Earning Referrals From Centers Of Influence

Chapter 9

The Ten Truths About High Net Worth Clients

By Frank Maselli

Q. *I want to focus on getting quality referrals to high net worth prospects. What suggestions can you provide to pursue this affluent market?*

My approach to referrals is not intended as a generic, all-client strategy. I believe you only want referrals from a small group of wealthy and influential clients and from centers of influence like CPAs and attorneys. A simple term to identify these types of clients is high net worth or HNW clients.

For these types of clients, the usual referral techniques don't work. I'm talking about techniques like:

"I need your help to grow my business, Bob".
"I get paid two ways."
"If you were me, Bob, how would you penetrate the physician community?"

Referrals take trust, and trust must be earned. It takes time to build trust in any relationship. Building it is a process that moves at a different pace for each person. The good news is that the process of developing referral-generating trust can be accelerated. You can actually start building a referral-based practice today, even on day one with a totally new client!

The ten truths

Before you can ask anyone for a referral, it helps to learn as much as possible about that person or that group in general. Here are my ten truths about HNW clients.

1. They know other people with similar needs and have influence with them - HNW clients move in various-sized circles into which you would love to be invited. They have influence or prestige in their worlds; and when they recommend you to a friend; that carries some weight.

2. They are hard to reach - To get into the world of the HNW client, it takes hard work, careful planning and a detailed understanding of who they are, what they need, how they think and who they know.

3. HNW clients want to feel special - Service goes way beyond the basics. It's going that extra mile and anticipating client needs and desires. And giving them things they didn't even know they needed or desired. It's proactive and customized.

4. HNW clients like working with winners and respect business success - They like to work with intelligent, successful professionals. It gives them the assurance that they're getting top-quality advice. Plus, they like to see a reflection of themselves when they look at you. Displaying success and confidence in the right way and professionally conveying a message of strength, skill and prosperity to your HNW clients is vital to the referral process.

5. They're busy - HNW clients are generally not thinking about you at all. To capture more referrals, you need to capture more real estate in their heads without being obnoxious.

6. They fear referrals and have a lot to lose - For HNW clients, referrals provide a tiny upside reward coupled with unlimited downside risk. It's this fear that prevents your best people from opening up their world to you in a meaningful way. If you want more referrals, you must make the fear go away, or at least minimize it sufficiently, to convince them that you will protect them from exposure and potential harm.

7. They are ferocious about privacy - Privacy and confidentiality are essential. They don't want anyone knowing anything about their finances, and they fear that you would divulge any information necessary to get a new client. You will hear them say, "I never get involved with my friends' finances." From their perspective, you must understand and appreciate this statement.

8. They admire your professional expertise - HNW clients like working with top-tier professionals in every industry that touches their lives. Develop a certain niche group of people whose needs you understand and are able to service completely. Become the "go to" advisor for that particular group, and find intelligent ways to spread the word of your expertise.

9. They don't know your story or how to tell it to others - Every day, your best clients are in a position to refer you to a friend or colleague, yet you say that they're not doing it. Why not? In many cases, it's because they don't really know you or what to say about you. They have no story to tell. Give clients the concepts and words to say when a referral opportunity presents itself. First, you need a clear message; then, you can tell it to the client. In fact, part of every conversation with a prospect needs to include a segment like this:

"Look, Bob. We know you have a dozen other advisors who want to help manage your money. At the core, we all have the same products, investment ideas and services. We may even have the same basic experience levels. Here is why you are going to love working with us."

It's worth spending as much time as necessary to come up with a consistent, compelling paragraph to follow that one.

10. HNW clients like a professional, customized approach - The way you ask for the referral will demonstrate the importance you place on the referral.

HNW clients don't generally respond well to the super-casual, laid-back, haphazard, random referral approach:
"So Bob, who else do you know that might be interested in retirement planning?"

They require a more formalized structure that recognizes the tremendous power they exert on others and the risks they run when using that power on your behalf.

Frank Maselli
President, The Frank Maselli Co. Inc.
Phone: 800-231-5272
Email: frank@frankmaselli.com
Website: www.maselligroup.com
Frank is the founder of The Maselli Group, a virtual team of training, coaching and marketing professionals. Our mission is to help financial advisors, wholesalers and managers master the advanced skills and attitudes needed for success in our new profession.

Chapter 10

Twelve Strategies For Getting High Net Worth Clients

By Frank Maselli

Q. *I want to pursue getting quality referrals to high net worth prospects. What suggestions can you provide to pursue this affluent market?*

These twelve strategies form a comprehensive approach to referrals that will change the way you do business. Start by developing a written Referral Plan. These referral generating activities start with a simple question: From which clients do you want referrals?

1. Identify twenty clients from whom you want referrals - Which of your clients are viable referral mining targets? Whom would you like to clone? You need to define this list and literally write the names on paper. You might have more than twenty clients in mind, but focus on, and start with, a small list because the effort necessary in this process could overwhelm you if you try too big a group. Look for the following criteria:

- Clients you really like. You want to build a business around great people about whom you truly care. This bond and good feeling becomes the cornerstone of the Strength Referral.

- Clients who truly value your expertise and who have potential influence with other people.

- Clients in growth industries where there is likely to be strong future potential business, such as lending, stock options and possibly investment banking.

- Clients in fast-changing or consolidating industries where there is potential for early retirement rollovers, transition 401(k) accounts, business sales or stock liquidations. In addition, look for clients who may interact with industries like this.

- Clients in niche industries that you might like to penetrate. Professionals who advise other wealthy or special needs folks. This includes the obvious centers of influence like accountants or attorneys, but can also include business managers, sports agents, top insurance executives who work with institutional clients and politicians.

2. Gather information - Take your list of 20 clients and build a Referral Intelligence File (RIF) on each one. Start by getting a loose leaf notebook about two inches thick.

Then, enlarge and print 40 copies of the sample page that follows. Using a loose leaf notebook allows you to add pages with articles, pictures, documents or other items you may find that help the process.

Name of Top Client

Personal World

Professional World

Community

Potential Referrals

The Referral Intelligence File® (RIF) worksheet

The purpose of the RIF is to look for links to prospective referrals. In the client's world, who might benefit most from your skill and advice? Who would you most likely enjoy having as a client?

- **Personal world**: Country clubs; hobbies; favorite vacation spots; people they socialize with; play tennis, golf, sail, travel, hunt or ski with; kids' or grandkids' names and schools; favorite restaurants or types of food and wine; who built their home; contractors they use; cars they drive; boats they own; planes they fly; dogs they show; horses they ride; art they collect; etc.

- **Professional world**: Names of colleagues, competitors, suppliers, clients, board memberships, certifications they have, trade publications they read, articles they've published, business books they write and read, meetings and conferences they attend, organizations they are in, etc.

- **Community**: Causes they support with time or money, clubs and civic organizations they join, charity events they host or attend, public activities they enjoy, groups they would like to participate in.

Look for specific links to the most important people in your client's life, the folks he/she cares about most deeply. The reason you are building this intelligence file is because top clients are way too busy to think of random people to refer to you. The generic question, "Who else do you know that might be interested in our services?" followed by the list of memory joggers is way too haphazard for these clients. It demonstrates no effort on your part and tells them that referrals are nothing more than an afterthought for you, an "Oh, by the way" sales tactic. Instead, you want to focus them immediately on a specific person. By targeting specific people in their world to whom you know they are connected, you channel their energies and demonstrate care, professionalism and preparation.

This approach is powerful; it works, and it makes you look serious and much more successful. You are selective about the people with whom you do business, and you take the time to know who they are before asking for a referral. That elevates your entire referral process a few notches in the client's mind.

3. Identify 20 top prospects you would like to meet - You start by gathering data on 20 top clients and searching for links to prospects. Now you're going to repeat the process with 20 top prospects and search for links to existing clients. Remember, referrals are a process, not a momentary snapshot conversation. Everything ties together to create a total referral approach, so this is only the first step. The most important parts here are the fact that you did your homework and went to the client with a specific name. You leave the client with the impression that you're a much more thorough professional and that you take referrals very seriously.

This intelligence gathering process is a career-long effort, but at some point within a month or so you will have created a thick binder filled with critical data on your top clients.

4. Provide excellent service - Every advisor's service model is slightly different, but great service is the baseline starting point for any referral process. High net worth (HNW) clients expect polished treatment, and your competition is giving it to them. Begin by conducting a thorough self-assessment of your service model followed up by an assessment from your top clients. Brutal honesty is the first step toward improving your efforts.

One of the philosophies that will help you manage client service expectations is an approach called "tough love." The core message here is that we are going to solve all client problems in a timely manner, but we're not going to drop everything and jump through hoops for routine requests.

As an example of tough love, I used to tell my clients that I handled all routine administrative requests on Fridays. Whenever someone would call in with a problem I would ask, *"How critical is this to you because if it's routine priority, I will have an answer for you by Friday. If it's critical, I will get it today."* Most of the time, they are fine with Friday. On those rare occasions when they needed an immediate answer, we would elevate the priority and get it done. Of course, we would strive to solve routine problems as fast as possible and actually get back to them by Thursday with an answer. Doing the Friday thing allowed me to manage expectations, train my clients, and provide my staff time to actually focus and get things done intelligently rather than rushing from fire to fire.

A quality many HNW clients seem to prize highly is the advisor's ability to anticipate needs, not just react to situations. For clients on your referral list, this anticipation will be one of the branding highlights they will mention to friends and colleagues when talking about you.

5. Position referrals from strength - You're a serious financial professional with unique and powerful skills. Without your help and guidance, thousands of HNW clients in your community will never reach their financial goals. This is a powerful reality that most advisors seem to forget when they ask for referrals. Let me give you a new metaphor for the referral approach that seems to be resonating with advisors out there. In my book I call it The Strength Referral and it goes like this:

- Our team is very successful and busy.

- These are confusing times for many people, and we are extremely concerned that many individuals are getting very bad advice and service.

- We've decided to open up our practice to a limited number of friends, colleagues and relatives of our top clients. Note the different tone – "We've decided to open up, limited number" - these convey scarcity, exclusivity, power - all things that top clients respect.

- You're one of them, and here's why we love you. It never hurts to occasionally tell your clients why you love them.

- We have limited capacity and want controlled growth. This allays one of the unspoken fears top clients have about referrals - that you will grow so big you won't give them the service they require.

- Anyone you love can access us now. This is about the people in your world you care for the most. In effect, you are saying, "Now that you're part of our family, we open our arms to anyone you care about."

- It's not about helping us growing our business. It's not our clients' jobs to help us grow. It's our job to help you and anyone you want to see saved.

- Referring people to us is very easy and safe, and here's how you do it. Walk them through the Referral Guide.

- Here's what we do when you refer someone. We handle your people with care and professionalism.

- Here are some people that we've identified in your world who you might want to think about. You are saying, "We've done all the homework for you, and we're very selective."

6. Stay top-of-mind - Your HNW clients are surrounded by people to whom you would love to be referred. However, those same clients are extremely busy people with their own set of concerns. Consequently they're not thinking about you. The goal is to stay on the client's personal radar screen in positive and creative ways that help them remember you exist and are worthy of referrals. I call this the 44 Touch System, meaning you must touch the client at least 44 times a year.

A touch can be almost anything including: phone calls, emails, newsletters, events, workshops, seminars, conference calls, webinars, hard copy research reports, white papers, and birthday and holiday cards. One of my favorite ideas is to send my top clients a subscription to National Geographic Magazine. Why National Geographic and not The Economist, Fortune, Forbes or Money? There are several reasons. First, National Geographic is a high quality magazine with award winning articles and photography. It's often something people keep for years so it has tremendous shelf life. It has nothing to do with money or investing, and so there will never be any conflicting advice. Because it's not business related, it sends a subliminal message about your desire to expand the relationship beyond the world of money.

Every client is different so the particular combination of touches will be customized for each one. Ideally, you can automate a few of these like emails and newsletters, so you don't have to manually control and oversee everything that's going on in the communication process. It should all be part of a coherent branding strategy that enhances your stature and reinforces your core message.

The bottom line in all this touching is to keep your story somewhere in the client's mind at all times. Make it as easy as possible for them to remember and refer you the next time one of their friends needs help. Empower them with knowledge, and arm them with specific messages to become your advocates in their circle of contacts.

7. Address the risks and emotions of referrals - HNW clients and centers of influence run huge personal and professional risks when referring friends, families and colleagues to you. These risks run the gamut from simple embarrassment to severe financial danger if you screw up doing something for someone they sent you. Only by making those risks go away can you expect significant referrals from your best people.

The first step in understanding this fear is to do a personal assessment and ask yourself some hard questions like: *"Do I fit in my client's world? Am I someone they could feel comfortable introducing to their best friends or colleagues?"*

The next step in reducing clients' apprehension is to show that you understand the risks the client faces when referring. I like to talk to the client about these risks of referrals, how things might go badly for them if I do something stupid. By addressing the risks honestly and openly, you are demonstrating a relationship sensitivity and personal awareness that most advisors don't possess. You climb quite a few notches in their mind. This gives you a chance to explain in detail how you handle referrals with extreme care and professionalism.

8. Target a specific industry or client niche - Becoming a specialist or an expert in some financial area or with certain specific types of clients will not only increase your referrals, but could become the cornerstone for your entire practice. It's a great way to focus your energy and direct your efforts toward ideas that intrigue you and people you are passionate about helping. To have any realistic claim of expertise in any subject, you need to have something in writing. So, why not start at the top of the credibility pyramid and write a book?

Another suggestion is in the realm of articles and interviews. Experts and specialists get published and interviewed. So you need to get something into your local newspaper, business journal or community bulletin. Ideally, you have found a niche market that has a trade publication for which you can write. Another option is to write a white paper that can be sent directly to your contacts via email or on your website. Create pieces that inform, entertain, empower and inspire people. Do not pitch products.

Getting some press can expand your business reach. Hiring a PR agent may be a great idea but can be pricey. Download the Personal Profile Interview from my website to learn of a more cost-effective strategy that could help.

This body of articles, interviews, white papers and perhaps books, verifies that you are a genuine expert and will help your best clients tell your story with tremendous impact. All of these pieces will go into your Referral Guide.

9. Build your brand identity - Building a brand identity, developing a compelling story, and learning to tell it well can make all the difference in your marketing and referral effort. However, even a great story won't get you any referrals unless the client can tell it to his/her friends. So build it for them to share.

What's your story? What do you want to be known for? What do you want your top clients to think and say about you to their friends and colleagues? Is this identity valuable and interesting to the clients you are seeking? Are your branding messages aligned with your natural strengths and behaviors? How are you going to get your branding message across in all your touches and actions? These questions are the start of the branding process, and they aren't easy to answer.

10. Use the new specialty referral - Chances are you've had some of your best clients for a very long time. They've come to know and trust you implicitly, and they are your perfect source for great referrals. But you might be reluctant to ask them because it upsets the long standing relationship dynamic. If you've never asked them for referrals before, you're changing the implied rules of the game as you've both played it for many years, and they may misinterpret your sudden request as a sign of business weakness.

The new specialty can be anything you like. Our profession is filled with exciting, new programs and solutions that can help people reach their goals. The key is that it's different from whatever you've been doing with that client before. The conversation might go like this:

"Bob, I wanted to talk to you about a special new service we've added to our practice over the past year. As you know,

a lot of folks are getting ready to retire; and they are facing a longer life span than any generation before in history. We've been encouraging many of our top clients to look at long term care issues mainly as a way to protect some of their retirement plan assets. I wanted to schedule a meeting to discuss this with you and thought it might be good if we could get some of the other attorneys in your office together for a little lunch session next week some time."

11. Use the event referral – HNW clients also love events and are very willing to bring their friends and colleagues if you give them something exciting, informative and entertaining to attend. That's not as easy as it might sound. Most events these days seem to be thinly disguised sales pitches for some product. If you can deliver real value, you will find that events can become not only a key part of your referral strategy, but the cornerstone of your entire practice.

Besides the fun of the social interaction, the event referral is also a low risk scenario for the client, because the referral gets to make the decision about you on his/her own. The client doesn't need to sell you, just the event. If you do a great session, the client looks good in the eyes of his/her friend. If you perform poorly, the client gets plausible deniability and can walk away relatively unscathed. The type of events you can do is limited only by your creativity and budget. Seminars are typical, but you can offer a host of lifestyle events such as cooking classes, spa days, golf outings, art gallery exhibitions, boat trips and health and wealth clinics. The list goes on. The internet has made possible a whole new form of virtual event marketing, so I would get comfortable with webinars and on-line workshops as well.

12. Use a Referral Guide - HNW clients and centers of influence want to know that you take referrals very seriously, and that when they give you a name, you are going to treat that person with extreme care and professionalism. Anything you can do to demonstrate that you understand this and will handle referrals in this way will improve the chances of getting great referrals from your best people.

A Referral Guide is a fantastic psychological positioning tool that sends all the right messages about the way you engage in the whole referral process. It also helps you to expand your clients' story-telling ability beyond a two sentence conversation fragment.

Frank Maselli

President, The Frank Maselli Co. Inc.
Phone: 800-231-5272
Email: frank@frankmaselli.com
Website: www.maselligroup.com
Frank is the founder of The Maselli Group, a virtual team of training, coaching and marketing professionals. Our mission is to help financial advisors, wholesalers and managers master the advanced skills and attitudes needed for success in our new profession.

Chapter 11

Creating A Referral Guide

By Frank Maselli

Q. *As part of a plan to get quality referrals to high net worth prospects, you suggested that I provide each referral source with his/her own Referral Guide. How do I create that?*

In basic form, a Referral Guide is nothing more than a three-ring binder. You're going to put information in it, and you need to have the words Referral Guide somewhere on the front cover. Binders generally have a very long shelf life and are stored somewhere visible like on a bookshelf. Binders are also easy to add things to. You should actually plan to update your binder periodically when you visit the client. That's a great way to create a new referral conversation as well.

The act of putting together a guide takes significant work. The Referral Guide is a stand-alone kit that deals specifically with the subject of referrals. If you have any marketing materials, you should probably create the Referral Guide with a similar look and feel to it, just to keep all your materials consistent. Your marketing brochure goes into the Referral Guide. Both pieces should complement and support each other.

The basic purpose of the Referral Guide is to upgrade or elevate the process of asking for referrals. It demonstrates that referrals are so important to you that you actually took the time to prepare an entire binder on the subject. With that, the client has something to fall back on. The guide becomes a tool he/she can use to tell your story. Or better yet, he/she can actually hand it to a friend and say, *"You should take a look at this. These guys are amazing!"*

The binder becomes your tangible presence in his/her office or home. Every time he/she sees it, it's going to remind him/her of you and the referral process. It is a remarkably simple yet powerful ally.

The best way to use your Referral Guide is in a face-to-face meeting with a top client over dinner or lunch. You need to have a little uninterrupted time. At this meeting, you are going to bring out the guide and actually walk the client through it, item by item, at a reasonable, but deliberate, pace. In doing so, you're trying to create the impression that you take referrals very seriously, and you've given the whole subject lots of careful thought.

What will the client do with the guide? Three possibilities are: 1) He/she may refer back to it periodically when thinking about referring you to someone. 2) He/she may actually give it to someone. In this way, the guide actually has two audiences, so you need to create it with that in mind, but your primary target is the existing client. 3) What's more likely, however, is that the client will stick the guide on a shelf and never look at it after that initial meeting. That's okay. It will still have done its job. The guide is a message transmitter or a state of mind creator. It will generate an amazing image in the client's head. In truth, you are building this guide mainly to facilitate a ten minute referral conversation that will last a lifetime.

What goes in the guide?

You can put almost anything you want in the guide, but there are a few items that you should definitely include. In general, avoid making it too bulky or cumbersome. Limit yourself to six to ten items at most so you can effectively walk the client through it in a single sitting without their eyes glazing over. Ideally the items you include should all fit neatly inside and actually look like they belong together. They should be professionally crafted without looking like they were created by your firm's marketing department. Make fresh copies. Use color. Personalize everything that speaks to the client. Remember, you're only going to be making ten or fifteen of these guides for your best clients so spend the time and effort to do them right.

Here's a description of suggested items to include in your guide. Each will be a tab in the binder. You may add or subtract as you see fit.

Referral Guide Tabs

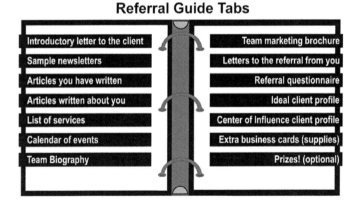

1. Introductory letter to the client - This is a personalized, one page letter that explains the overall philosophy of referrals and addresses the two biggest fears the client has about the referral process. You're going to be talking through much of this philosophy, but the letter is a hard-copy reminder of what you said with some augmentations built in for future reference.

A sample letter

Heading
Dear Bob:

I'm writing to thank you for allowing the Maselli Group to manage your investment and financial portfolio. We appreciate the trust you've placed in us, and we're eager to help you reach your financial goals. As you know, the investment world today can be complex and confusing.

Recently, my partners and I have become very concerned that there are many investors out there who may not be getting the kind of quality attention and personal guidance they need. In that light, we've decided to open our practice to the personal referrals of our top clients.

As one of those top clients, our commitment to you extends to anyone in your world about whom you care deeply. That might include family members, friends or colleagues. Within that broad circle, it's possible that you may know someone who would appreciate our kind of personalized service or benefit from some of our insights concerning their investments.

If that's true, you should know two things. First, my team and I treat all referrals with the utmost care and discretion. Your referrals will receive the very best service and personalized attention. Their experience with the Maselli Group will be positive, highly professional and will reflect very well upon you. Second, we maintain a strict policy of complete confidentiality. At no time will I or anyone on my staff discuss your portfolio or financial situation with anyone.

It may seem unnecessary to state these points so directly; but we value your referrals a great deal, and I want you to know how seriously we take them. They are, in fact, the only way we accept new clients.

Thank you for the opportunity to be of service. We look forward to working with you.

Sincerely,
Frank Maselli

This letter is simply a mini-form of the Strength Referral we discussed earlier. It also addresses the two big fears of embarrassment and confidentiality.

2. Sample newsletters - They're one of the simplest and most impactful tools you can use in your practice. Ideally you are able to write your own, but in lieu of that a firm-created piece is fine. Put one or two past issues of your newsletter in the guide. If you're not using a newsletter now, I urge you to examine that strategy. You are competing with other advisors who do, and you're eventually going to lose that battle.

3. Articles you've written - If you can write articles or have access to ghostwritten ones, you should think about this as part of your overall marketing strategy. People who write stuff are smart, important, and serious members of their professions who command respect and authority beyond the average competitor.

4. Articles written about you - One of the greatest things you can do for your business is to get some ink, some positive press about you and your team. There are a number of ways to get the right kind of press, and I have recommended that several top advisors get help from a good PR agent. That can be pricey however, so I've developed a powerful alternative or first step to PR called The Personal Profile Interview. You can download information and a sample of this from my website. The advisors who have used the PPI have told me it's the greatest marketing thing they've ever done.

5. List of services - Most clients probably know less than ten percent of your capabilities. Their perceptions are a very narrow slice of your total pie. Many times, they are hesitant to refer you because they think their friends would not need the same advice or investment programs you gave them. So show them the whole spectrum of what you do. You can always narrow down the parameters later. Initially, this will help you cast a broader net for potential referrals. On your List of Services, you might want to include three sections:

- Things you specialize in

- Things your firm can do

- Things you can refer a client to

Depending on your market, you can include a whole host of ancillary professional services from aircraft loans to golf pros to hospice care providers.

6. Calendar of events - Holding events for your clients is a tremendous way to boost referrals. So, in the kit, you want to include a complete listing of dates, times, and locations of all the events you have planned for the year and beyond. I always like to throw in one or two things that are at least a year or two down the road. A calendar like this not only gives people time to prepare, but it also sends positive, subliminal messages about you:

- You're organized. You plan things in advance and think them through, both of which are good characteristics.

- You're going to be here for the long haul. You're part of the community and plan to be part of your clients' lives for many years to come.

- You're a busy professional. You have lots of activities going on and plan months, if not years, in advance.

7. Team biography or marketing brochure - Everyone on your team gets a biography. You may also want to include people who you may not normally think of as part of your team. Some examples are business coaches, great wholesalers who bring value to your business, your managers and other professionals who regularly work with your clients. This is where you get to create a virtual team of specialists and experts who can be brought in on certain cases to solve problems. The goal is to let the client know that you are ready and able to address a broad array of their potential needs.

8. Introductory letter to the referral from you - You might send this letter to a referral when a client gives you a name. You show this letter to the client as a way of relaxing him/her about your approach.

A sample letter

> *Dear Referral:*
>
> You have probably never heard of The Maselli Group, but one of our top clients and a mutual friend suggested that I drop you a line. Bob Smith of Allied Chemical thought that you might be intrigued by some of the unique services and ideas we have developed for use with executives such as yourself.
>
> ---
>
> *A simple opening that tells the referral where you got his name and piques his curiosity with the words "intrigued" and "unique services.*
>
> ---
>
> We've worked with Bob for several years and built a great relationship of trust with him and his family over that time. Our practice is very selective, and we work only by referral with a small handful of top executives in the community. Bob is one of our favorite people, and he thinks very highly

of you. So I am writing to introduce myself.

Give a little history about you and Bob, but obviously no investment details. This could be tweaked for a different kind of referral such as a corporate account or a 401(k).

I would enjoy a chance to talk with you about some of the things we can do at the Maselli Group and how those strategies might positively impact your financial and investment needs today or potentially down the road. Bob also mentioned that you enjoy an occasional round of golf. I'd like to invite you to join me at the Raleigh Country Club on Wednesday the 12th or Saturday the 15th of June. If neither of those dates works, we may be able to flex around your schedule. I will call your office later this week to touch base.

This is the action step. This paragraph can be switched out with others as the specific circumstances apply.

Best regards,
Frank Maselli

The body of this letter will remain fairly constant, but I might change the action step, depending on the circumstances of the case. For example, this might be an alternative ending:

Bob also mentioned that you might enjoy attending one of our Strategic Insight dinners at the Capital Grill. Our next event is on June 23rd at 7 p.m. and will feature a portfolio manager for one of the top money management firms in the industry. This might give us a chance to chat and for you to see a bit more about what we do here at Maselli Group. These are usually very enjoyable and insightful events. I'm sure Bob can tell you more about them.

I will call your office later this week to touch base.

You might want to include two or three letters in your Referral Guide, each with a slightly different ending, and let the client choose the one he feels most comfortable with.

9. The ideal client profile - This is a one-page document you would prepare to let the client know the kinds of prospective referrals you are looking for. You can make it broad and general or narrow and detailed depending on the type of practice you're trying to build or message you want to send to that specific client.

For example, if you're giving this to a business owner, you might want to focus on entrepreneurs or other people he is most likely to know. So maybe you keep 80 percent of it the same and only customize 20 percent for the client. Personally, I like to keep this simple. My own Ideal Client Profile is designed to uncover the exact type of client I truly love.

Sample letter to profile my ideal client

At the Maselli Group, we work with investors who care deeply about the important things in life, and who find joy in places far more permanent than beating the S&P 500, achieving a lower portfolio standard deviation or being invested in the hot asset class of the week.

We work with those investors who realize that navigating this ocean of noise and confusion on the way to a more secure and enjoyable life is a difficult journey that will require discipline, patience and planning. But that given those attributes, along with a sense of irony and humor, we will most assuredly get there and have fun along the way.

We work with investors who understand that tomorrow is always brighter and that the markets, while temporarily out of balance, are ultimately a measure of the unlimited human spirit. They seek to participate in that incredible experience over multiple lifetimes for themselves and their progeny.

Finally we work with people who recognize the value in using professional, skilled, trained and caring advisors to guide them on that journey and who are willing to pay a fair price for that help.

If you know anyone like this, we would be pleased to talk with them.

10. Center of influence ideal client profile - This is a page you fill out for each of your partner CPAs, attorneys and other professionals to find out who their ideal clients may be. As a document, it's very simple, basically a blank note sheet with the words "Bob's Ideal Clients" written on top.

You will use it in an interview with the CPA to learn about their practice.

There has always been an unspoken quid pro quo between several related professions in the financial field i.e. You give me referrals, and I give you referrals. That arrangement works well and is beneficial to all parties. What you are doing with this profile is taking that informal agreement and making it more official and professional. I might say something like this to a C.P.A.:

"Jack, we are obviously in a position to help each other here. I have clients who will need accounting help at some point, and I would like to be able to refer them to you. Take a few minutes and tell me a little about your practice. What kinds of clients are you looking for, and how can I help you find them?"

This interview process will elevate your stature in the mind of the CPA or center of influence in a very meaningful way. It lets them know that you are a careful professional who takes referrals very seriously and that you are real partner who is genuinely interested in their success as well as your own. It's a two-way street.

You can also use this interview idea with a wide array of folks beyond the traditional referral sources you may have considered. Think about all the professionals who deal with HNW clients in some way. Find the ones who work with the kinds of clients you might like and who could also benefit from referrals from you. This list can include people from what I call the service professions such as accountants, attorneys, business managers, sports or theatrical agents, insurance agents, etc.

Then take a look at the "lifestyle professions" such as golf and tennis pros, restaurant owners, personal trainers, boat and airplane brokers, car sales people, stable owners, dog breeders, hunting and fishing guides, clothing salespeople, home contractors and travel agents. These lifestyle folks may not be as close to the actual finances as the service people, but they do occupy a position of trust in the life of your potential referral.

Think creatively, and keep your eyes open for opportunities to link up with other top professionals with whom you can share ideas and services. After they prove themselves to be reliable, you might add them to your virtual team and make them part of your overall service model.

11. Supplies - Be sure you to include a small supply of business cards in your Referral Guide. Put them in a nice card case or holder that keeps them neat and looking professional.

That's it for the Referral Guide. You can add or subtract items as you see fit. Keep it simple enough to walk the client through it in a single sitting.

Frank Maselli

President, The Frank Maselli Co. Inc.

Phone: 800-231-5272

Email: frank@frankmaselli.com

Website: www.maselligroup.com

Frank is the founder of The Maselli Group, a virtual team of training, coaching and marketing professionals. Our mission is to help financial advisors, wholesalers and managers master the advanced skills and attitudes needed for success in our new profession.

Chapter 12

Acquiring Referrals And Warm Introductions

By C. Richard Weylman

Q. *I want to increase my success with the affluent and wealthy. How can I get more referrals for that target market?*

Acquiring referrals is an important channel to growing your business, but gaining an introduction or bridge is the key. That's because the introduction enables you to actually reach the referral. Why are referrals coupled with introductions so important? Three referrals typically result in one sale. So the more referrals and introductions you get, the more traction, the more penetration, the more income and the more opportunity you experience. This is a brilliant way to build a business.

Here are the principles that will insure a successful referral and warm introduction system.

1. Recognize that most clients do not know how to qualify a prospect - Only you know the type of people you want as clients. So when you ask clients if they know of anyone who could use some financial advice, their thought is that everyone they know already has an advisor.

2. Get in charge of your business - Know what you want and where you want to grow. You want an introduction to the right people, people you have pre-qualified in your vertical or targeted market. You've done the research in advance by identifying a list of names of high quality prospects in your market.

3. You are seeking a bridge or introduction to reach pre-qualified people - Instead of asking for names, you provide the client with names of specific targeted people whom they are likely to know in their market. Then, the client can give you insight on how you can be introduced to the prospect or how to connect.

The pre-qualified list shows clients that you have direction in your business and that you are focused. It links to prospects whom the client may know and to existing relationships in their vertical markets. Also, the list creates awareness that you know and want to know people just like themselves. This reinforces the client's sense of well-being and belonging. Last, providing your clients with a list of names stimulates them to think vertically so that they can introduce you to more people like them. To be effective, research every name.

Present the client with no more than 15 names. Why 15? I've taken 25, and it's too many. Usually the client wants you to leave the list if it's too long. I want the client to review the list while I'm sitting with him/her, not leave it behind. And, if I take only five or ten names, I imply that I need more. After clients have reviewed the list, ask them who was omitted. At this point, they're thinking about people by market, not trying to simply come up with random names.

4. Have a consistent process - By providing clients with solid targets for growing your business to the next level, you are growing where you want to go! Be proactive - such as giving them ideas on how to meet (breakfast, lunch, dinner, golf outings, go to a sporting event, etc.), knowing your calendar in advance and setting specific follow-up times to call back.

5. You need to know when to ask for introductions from clients - There are four great opportunities: when you close the sale, when you gain an account, when you deliver the policy or paperwork, or when you conduct a review.

6. Always send a thank you note to anyone who provides an introduction or referral - This is critically important because it keeps clients "in the know." They can continue to influence their friends. Don't send a gift, just a thank you note.

7. Finally, here are some tips for implementing your process -
- Adjust your mindset. Expect referrals and warm introductions to help you meet qualified people.

- Start managing your calendar four to five weeks in advance so you know the days and the events where you can play golf, go to lunch or take prospects to sporting/cultural/theater type events. Keep your company marketing events in mind as well. Allocate at least 20 to 30 percent of your week to these marketing activities. This is useful in your networking activities as well. It is critical that you spend much time outside of the office if you wish to cultivate leads.

- Start creating lists of 15 prospects now. Then, invest in the services of a marketing intern or high school student to assist you. Specifically, get creative in your thinking as you put together lists of new prospects. Research the list thoroughly to be sure the individuals are qualified. Track your calendar carefully so that you can attend events and invite the people you want to meet.

- Create an action plan to log the steps that you will take to begin the introduction process so that you're not just getting referrals, but you're getting introductions.

C. Richard Weylman

Chairman, Weylman Consulting Group
Phone: 941-928-3600
Email: Richard@richardweylman.com
Website: www.richardweylman.com

Richard helps others understand today's marketplace, and elevate business performance. He is the author of the bestselling book, *Opening Closed Doors — Keys to Reaching Hard to Reach People* and the founder of The Weylman Center For Excellence™ In Practice Management, an online Marketing Support Center and university for professionals and staff to elevate their business performance in today's marketplace.

Chapter 13

How To Get Comfortable Asking For Referrals

By Matt Anderson

Q. *I want to build my practice by getting referrals. How can I get comfortable asking for them?*

There is a basic layer of confidence that needs to be established if you're going to effectively ask for referrals.

1. You only ask for referrals if you've earned them - Too much of what we hear about referrals is based around techniques: how to ask, when to ask, what to say and who to get them from. We don't spend enough time focusing on what we are actually doing to earn the word-of-mouth recommendation. Neither you nor your clients recommend someone unless they deserve it, unless something truly valuable in the other person's eyes has been delivered. Expectations must be exceeded. If you have only done your job, you cannot expect someone to tell others.

Part of your referral conversation should include a discussion about what your client has gotten out of working with you. This will tell you whether you should be asking. This is the first layer. If you have brought value, this makes asking much easier.

2. Understand why people refer you - Andy Sernovitz's research at Northwestern University has found that that there are two main reasons why people refer others. First, referring you to other people in their life makes *them* feel good. Second, they like to help people *they* care about. Notice neither of these reasons has anything to do with YOU. It's not about you; it's about them.

They are motivated about what's important to *them*. Knowing this can build your confidence because now you don't have to fear looking needy – their world does not revolve around you! It revolves around people who *they* would like to help – who are also hopefully good prospects for you.

The second layer then in building your confidence is making sure your referral request focuses on how your happy client might be able to help others. It's not a conversation about how you grow your business because most of the time other people do not care about this.

3. Have empowering beliefs about asking for referrals - When it comes to asking for referrals, most people believe that they are being pushy by asking or that it makes them look needy if they are asking. You must ask yourself what concerns you have about asking.

Your beliefs create your reality. Unfortunately, 87 percent of the thoughts we have are unconscious ones – habitual thoughts that are mostly negative and unhelpful. The solution is to change your beliefs by coming up with one that empowers you to ask. Provided your client recognizes that you have brought value and you ask in a way that's about your client helping others, fears you have about looking pushy or cheesy are completely unfounded.

The biggest difference between people who get many referrals and those who don't is that the successful ones think differently. They have mostly empowering beliefs about asking for referrals that encourage them towards what they want. The most empowering belief you can have about getting referrals is this: I'm good at what I do. I can help people you care about and I know I need to ask you!

One exercise I recommend is to list 20 reasons why someone should do business with you. You have to become your number one fan. For some advisors, this is where the light bulb goes on and a third layer of confidence is built. Simply putting in some time thinking hard about the value that you bring to the table can make a significant difference. It compares to when you first started in the business and were unsure at times about what you were saying, hoping nobody would ask you a question you didn't know the answer to. Think back to that time and remember also that at some later date you were in a meeting and consciously realized that all those doubts had gone because you did know your stuff! You were making eye contact with assurance. That's the kind of transition you can experience with asking for referrals as well.

Warning: Be ready for your brain to resist change. Your unhelpful beliefs are not going to be substituted without a fight. Amazingly, our habitual thoughts are 1,000 times stronger than a new one. Even when your status quo is unhelpful, your brain will still fight to keep you in this so-called comfort zone.

4. Pre-plan your asks - A fourth layer of confidence will be there if you go into a meeting knowing what your referral request is. What door would you like opened by your happy client? This is an incredibly important habit to develop. Then you don't spend time distracted during the meeting wondering who to ask for.

If your initial response to this idea is "I often don't know who they know," then you first need to develop the habit of what I call 'fishing'. During your time with that client, fish for people who are important in their life and who they like. Who do they know that might make a good prospect for you? You can't expect them to figure this out on the spot, so your conversation should include this activity.

5. Know when the best time is to ask for referrals - The best time to ask is when your client is most happy with your work. Clearly that is when he or she will go to bat for you most enthusiastically. The only thing that complicates this topic is your self-doubt. Again, if your client recognizes that you have brought value, it is okay to ask.

An even better time is after such a meeting when you have stopped talking business and are just chatting about something light, pleasant and more personal. People relax at this time, and it feels more natural and less formal to bring up a referral request as an "after-thought". This works well and psychologically feels right too.

Matt Anderson
The Referral Authority
Phone: 312-622-3121
Email: matt@thereferralauthority.com
Website: www.thereferralauthority.com
International author and speaker, Matt helps business people expand their marketing territory by mastering the art of business referrals. Matt is the author of Fearless Referrals™ – How to Ask in a Way That's Comfortable for YOU and Market Yourself For Free.

Chapter 14

Pursuing Financial Planners As Lead Sources

By Rhonda Vry-Bills

Q. *I need more quality leads. How can I successfully pursue financial planners and other trusted advisors as lead sources?*

Pursuing financial planners and other trusted advisors is a very effective way to develop a large network of lead referral sources. I successfully transitioned from selling LTCI over the phone and through the mail as a salaried employee to starting my own business as an independent agent who was dependent upon generating my own leads and doing personal face-to-face production.

Here's what I suggest you do:

1. Start by compiling a list of those who serve as trusted advisors to clients - It should include financial planners; estate planning attorneys; banks; employers; and brokers and insurance agents, including health, life, disability and

P&C. The goal is to convert the names on the list into profitable referral sources.

2. Don't spend a lot of money on marketing materials - At the end of the day, it's mostly about the handshake and the trusted and valued relationship that you develop with that professional advisor. I spend more time up front with the advisor. I spend time getting to know who he/she is, who the clients are, how the advisors meet with their clients and what advisors' needs are when working with their clients.

We can't help people if we don't know what their situation is; when working with other advisors, it is important to understand their roles with their own clients.

3. Let the business advisors know that they don't need to know all of the carriers and policy features - Instead, you will teach them to identify good prospects and how to schedule an appointment with you. Suggest that they mention LTC insurance the next time they deliver the life policy, do an annual review or review an auto policy.

Advisors can use this mini-script: *"I was looking through your file. Who do you have your long term care insurance with?"* If they have it, great. Ask them to provide a copy of their policy and offer to have a specialist review it for free. Also, that advisor can now have a copy for the files in the event the kids call one day. If the client does not have a policy, suggest that the advisor inform the clients that they need to set a time to discuss the protection.

4. Leave some materials that the advisor can use when discussing LTCI with the client - Create a folder and explain the contents to the advisor. Discuss which of their clients are good LTCI prospects, i.e., those who are over age 40, over $40K in income, white collar, couples, divorced, widowed, last kid graduating from college and self-employed. Specifically, I share the reasons why LTCI planning is crucial for each of these client categories. Provide a sheet so advisors can start writing down names as you go through the categories, because you know they are already thinking of some of their clients.

5. Spend time getting to know new referring clients by asking numerous questions to determine how to best meet their needs - What are their experiences with LTCI? Have they have written any policies? Find out how many requests do they get; and when they do, what do they normally do? Who are their clients? What is the majority of their business? Do their clients come to their office, or do they travel to their home? How many people are in their office? Is the referring advisor a one-man shop or do office assistants handle the administration?

6. Explain that LTCI is a rapidly changing product in plan designs, carriers, underwriting, forms and tax regulations - Tell advisors that if they're not staying on top of LTCI all the time, they may encounter problems. If you are an LTCI specialist, emphasize that you provide peace of mind, explain that LTCI is all you do and they do not have to view you as a threat.

7. Share the commissions 50/50 - Most advisors will realize this is an advantageous arrangement, since you do all of the work and they just have to recognize which clients need LTCI and schedule the appointment.

8. I like to dare the advisor to come up with the first client - For example, suggest a farmer or self-employed/business owner; now you can help educate the advisor about the tax deductions. Always start with the path of least resistance.

Once an advisor gets that first check, it will be a lot more inviting for him/her to think of the next client. You may want to give the advisor an additional incentive for the first paid case, such as a $50 card, or an additional gift for their fifth paid case.

Your initial goal should be to find 20 good referring advisors. Not all of them will refer leads, but just keep planting the seeds by continually keeping in contact, particularly when they are not referring. Keep your face and name in front of them. Find reasons to stop by their office, such as providing new tax guidelines, a new brochure or a table tent. Continue to network in order to get more advisors.

Try to make everything as easy as possible for the referring advisor. If he/she can refer a lead to you and not have to deal with details, he/she will be a lot more eager to hand you another referral.

My final words of advice are, "Be patient." If you believe in what you are doing, it will work. Just like any other business, you will have some referral sources that will feed you leads constantly and others sporadically. Either way, keep in front of them, keep your name there and when they do have a case they will contact you first.

Rhonda Vry-Bills, CLTC

President and CEO of Long Term Care Strategies, Inc.
Phone: 515-957-9333
Email: RhondaBillsLTC@aol.com
Website: www.ltcistrategies.com
Rhonda Bills specializes exclusively in Long Term Care planning with over 16 years in the industry. She works with a broad range of professionals who need her area of expertise.

Chapter 15

Partnering With Financial Advisors

By Denise Gott

Q. *Partnering with financial advisors and other professional advisors like CPA's and attorneys is an extremely effective way to tap into qualified prospects. How do you suggest I accomplish this?*

More and more financial advisors are realizing the need for long term care planning for their clients, yet advisors are not inclined to dive into the complicated web of this product. Advisors are looking for expert advice to assist their clients in making informed decisions on LTC insurance planning while protecting their book of business. LTC specialists are uniquely positioned to provide this expertise and add value to the advisor's practice.

Most advisors have very close relationships with their clients, which often translates into much warmer, more qualified prospects. The process of partnering with financial advisors and insurance professionals is simple, yet specific in the steps you should follow to make the relationship work.

The five-step system to developing successful, strategic partnership relationships with financial advisors, insurance professionals and other centers of influence works like this:

Step 1 - Get the advisors to know, like and trust you. It's a known fact that people do business with people they like. Start by having a well prepared agenda with probing questions to ask the advisor during your first appointment.

This will help you interact with the advisors and gain a good understanding of their personalities, business structures and goals. Use the advisors' names throughout the conversation to keep them engaged. Eye contact is critical in building trust. Establish that your primary intent is to help the advisors build and protect their clients and subsequently their book of business. Take notes during your interview so that you can summarize your conversation at the end of the meeting. These notes will also help you in your follow-up conversations with the advisors.

Step 2 - Your list of questions should focus on the advisors. Go into the meeting with a list of specific questions to learn from the advisors what is most important to them about providing LTC protection for their clients. Don't just ask questions from a list, though. Be sure to expand on each question and let the conversation flow. Find out how long they have been in the business. Learn about their philosophies, beliefs and even when they plan to retire. Ask probing questions such as: "What is the primary focus of your practice: business owners, individuals, financial planning, mutual funds, stocks and bonds? What is the average age of your clients? How many clients do you have? What is the minimum net worth of your clients?" Write everything down! Your notes will enable you to formulate an effective plan that helps advisors discover that helping their clients obtain LTCI is essential to building a strong practice.

Step 3 - Find out what type of experience the advisors have had with long term care. There may be personal experiences that will support your efforts to develop working relationships. Focus this segment of your visit on educating the advisors. Share some statistics on the risks of needing long term care, the cost of care in the region and the potential impact on a client's financial plan should the need for long term care arise.

Help the advisor to realize that denial is a huge factor in the lack of planning on the part of their clients. Be prepared to handle objections. Many advisors haven't learned about the risks associated with long term care themselves, and therefore, hold many of the same beliefs as a client.

They may even ask you to give your presentation for them, thereby, offering you an opportunity not only to demonstrate your skill, but also to educate the advisor about this issue. A word of caution: Don't be over zealous in attempting to sell the advisor during your first interview.

That will come later. Many advisors wind up purchasing LTCI as a result of a good, strong strategic partnership.

Step 4 - Present the solution by explaining your commitment to LTC planning through a comprehensive educational process and by creating a customized plan for every client. The advisor will begin to realize that you are the solution. Your expertise and dedication to working exclusively in the LTC market brings value to the trusted advisors' practice. Emphasize your focus on planning and your access to a wide variety of LTC products, tailored to suit each individual client.

By now you should have some indication as to whether or not the advisors are interested in working with you. Before you leave your first appointment with an advisor, indicate your intent to develop a strategic plan to market LTCI and that you would like to set a second appointment to present the plan. Begin by laying out a plan of action that gives the advisors a few different activities from which to choose. Your intent is to obtain agreement on one or two of these activities during your second visit; otherwise, you'll never get started.

Step 5 - Ask the advisors to arrange meetings with a few clients, so that you can demonstrate your skills and professionalism. Invite the individual advisor to sit in on the educational presentation with the client. This will further build trust and give the advisor a chance to observe how you interact with his clients.

Another way to get started might be to introduce you as the LTC specialist for XYZ Financial Services Company, via a letter from the advisor. Have a sample of this letter in your folder. Another possibility is to meet with the advisor and the client when the advisor holds a quarterly or annual review of a client's portfolio. If you give the advisor simple language to use, you will make him comfortable with the process.

At some point, you will have to address commission splits. A fair method is to use the Million Dollar Round Table (MDRT) split agreement which divides commissions based on who does the case work. Five categories make up the MDRT split agreement; and in most cases, you can create a split arrangement that is mutually agreeable to you and the advisor.

You may complete these five steps in two or three meetings with the individual advisor. Follow up is critical. Always stay ahead of the advisor by using articles, emails, sales tools and occasional telephone calls. Advisors will appreciate receiving ongoing information and know that you are committed to a long term, mutually beneficial, strategic partnership.

Denise Gott, MBA, CLTC

Senior Sales Leader for LTC Financial Partners
Phone: 440- 461-5131
Email: denise@ltcfp.net
Website: www.denisegott.ltcfp.com
Denise has over 15 years of experience in long term care insurance sales and serves on the Board of Directors of LTCFP.

Chapter 16

Getting Referrals From Property And Casualty Agents

By Tobe Gerard

Q. *What suggestions can you provide to generate quality leads by partnering with Property and Casualty (P&C) agents?*

Most of my referrals come from P&C insurance agents. Here are some helpful hints that will make partnering with these professionals easier.

1. The first thing to know is that P&C agents function in a crisis-oriented environment that lends itself more to reactive than proactive behavior. In their world, they are always putting out fires. Thus many P&C agents have no free time to be mining their clients for LTCI.

2. Second, be aware that P&C agents are extremely possessive about their book of business. Many P&C agencies are family-run businesses that are now in their third generation. These agents usually live in the town where their

agency is located. They have great integrity and pride themselves on knowing everything about their clients. As a result, they are extremely hesitant to allow outsiders to work with their clients. They fear that an outsider may behave inappropriately and perhaps ruin the relationship that they have spent years developing. As a result of this mindset, you will need to proceed very slowly and do whatever it takes to establish that you are trustworthy. For your initial meeting, you may want to consider putting together a folder that provides a P&C agent with the following:

- Your biography

- A list of local professionals who presently refer their clients to you

- A page of testimonials from referring professionals

- A list of ways that you differentiate yourself from others who sell LTCI

- A simple brochure or one page explanation of LTCI

- A recent article on LTCI that is positive

3. When starting a conversation with a P&C agent about why they should be offering LTCI, show them both the upside of making LTCI available to their clients as well as the downside if they don't. The most obvious downside is that they could lose their client to another P&C agent who offers LTCI. The harsh reality is that if they aren't offering this line of insurance to their clients, someone else will. P&C agents have already been schooled in the benchmarks of "total account selling" and "account rounding," so

remind them gently that selling LTCI is an integral part of these practices.

4. The other downside has malpractice implications. If a P&C agent's "Yellow Page" ad says that they offer "Life and Health Insurance" or "Life and Financial Services," make them aware of a potential E&O pitfall. If they're advertising that they offer these lines and yet are not selling LTCI to their clients who have assets to protect, it means that they are allowing their valued clients to go bare when LTCI would help them protect their nest egg.

Benefit to a P&C agent

The benefit to a P&C agent if they do offer LTCI is they will now have an additional revenue stream. In a down economy, where their commissions are being cut and their employees want an equitable raise every year, they will be receptive to hearing about an opportunity to add thousands of dollars to their bottom line with very little work on their part.

Familiarize yourself with their website. During your initial meeting, let them know that you had a chance to review their website and that you were able to learn a lot about their business. Share with them that there are at least two categories of their clients for whom LTCI would be a good fit: their clients who own personal umbrella coverage and those who own a business.

For their personal umbrella clients, have a letter already prepared to leave behind. The letter would:

- Compliment the client on purchasing personal umbrella coverage to protect their assets. Focus on how in today's litigious society it's important that their assets are protected properly. Remind them that owning a personal umbrella is a great safety net if something goes wrong and the goal of this coverage is peace of mind - personal umbrella coverage starts where other liability insurance ends.

- Make the analogy that LTCI also protects assets and provides peace of mind. It too starts where other insurances like health insurance and even Medicare end.

- It's a great safety net should something go wrong and there is a need for long term care.

For their clients who own a business, you would want to have another letter already prepared. The letter would focus on the area of deductibility, as well as the concept of being able to discriminate and provide LTCI for a particular "class" of employees. A P&C agent knows which clients own businesses that are struggling and which own businesses that are profitable and ripe for LTCI.

I wish I could tell you that you will gain a P&C agent's trust with very little work on your part, but that is not true. These professionals barely have time to run their own businesses. You will have to be highly motivated because you will need to spend a tremendous amount of time and energy to establish your credibility. It will be your job to make the relationship with a P&C agent as easy and as turnkey as possible.

Tobe Lynn Gerard, CLTC, MBA, MLS

President, Tobe Gerard Insurance, LLC
Phone: (508) 653-8110
Email: TGerard@TobeGerardInsurance.com
Website: tobegerardinsurance.com
Tobe has run her own business as a LTCI specialist for the past 13 years. Prior to that, she spent 20 years working for a P&C trade association.

Chapter 17

Cultivating Referral Sources
With Effective Drip Marketing
By Marilee Driscoll

Q. *How can I continually "touch" my referral sources so that they will provide me with leads?*

Most agents have had the experience of meeting a potentially great referral source that fizzled – perhaps because they didn't manage to keep in touch effectively. To increase your credibility visibility with professional referral sources, implement an effective, ongoing drip marketing system. The system that I am outlining here has worked for both captive agents and brokers for more than ten years.

Here are the steps:

1. Get or write meaningful content for monthly communication - The backbone of the system is having something meaningful - either entertaining or educational for the specific audience - to say each month. What you say to them must show that you are a credible, thoughtful professional for LTC planning and insurance.

Your communication to prospective and existing referral sources must be original; it cannot look like the typical promotional piece or sales letter.

You can write this piece yourself, outsource it to a ghostwriter, or subscribe to a service. Remember though, if you use a ghostwriter, you will still be responsible for coming up with a story angle each month. Other options include sending a company piece such as a generic tax guide or a magazine article reprint. (Photocopies or scanned PDFs violate US Copyright law unless you have specific permission).

2. Identify 50 to 100 referral sources that you will Drip Market to each month - Compile a list of viable referral sources such as estate planning and/or elder law attorneys, financial planners, tax preparers including CPAs and enrolled agents, benefit brokers or other occupations that you believe have potential. My experience and the experience of the many LTC agents with whom I regularly work indicates that individuals in the LTC caregiving industry are not a good referral source.

3. Include a fax-back response ("call-to-action") form and web-based landing page - Faxes may seem to be a thing of the past; however, fax-back forms are very effective since they will hold it in their hand and it reminds the referral source to communicate with you. Your primary communication should include a short compelling biography and your contact information, and both should be printed on white paper.

Make the fax-back form a different color and include your email address, phone number, an easy-to-type in response URL, as well as a list of reasons why the recipient should contact you. These reasons could include: 1) I have a client who needs long term care insurance, 2) I would like to sponsor a program for an organization on planning for long term care, or 3) I have a policy that needs to be reviewed.

4. Work the system - Assuming that you complete nothing but the monthly mailings, generally it takes three to six months to see results. Some agents have gotten referrals in month one, but, as the fine print on weight loss program ads read, those "results are not typical."

By attending association and/or networking meetings with recipients, and/or following up with telephone calls, you can turbo-charge your results.

Incorporate your photo into the monthly mailing so you become recognizable. Your goal in any networking situation is to add people to your monthly mailing…if they have seen your photo you will make this happen sooner.

Warning - These common mistakes will kill the effectiveness of your drip marketing:

- Do not use regular letterhead or your regular business envelopes. To increase the odds of your mail being opened, use a large, flat envelope with no company name or credentials on the return address.

- Do not mention particular insurance companies. This sounds like a sales pitch.

- Do not send email to professionals who you haven't met, and never send your communication as a PDF attachment. People do not read email from unknown individuals, and even people who know you don't want to have to click on a PDF to open your writing. Email your communication only after the prospective recipient knows you and has given his or her permission to receive your monthly article via email.

Marilee Driscoll

Creator of the LTC drip marketing program called the *Driscoll Drip.*
Phone: 508-830-9975
Email: md@marileedriscoll.com
Website: www.ltcsalestools.com
Marilee's Driscoll Drip marketing program has made it easy for producers and general agencies to raise credibility and visibility with professional referral sources, business owners and media. Driscoll is an author, speaker, columnist and a marketing and PR consultant to the LTC insurance industry.

Chapter 18

Using Pinging To Get Referrals And To Build Relationships

By Annette Bau

Q. **I want to create an ongoing flow of referrals. How can I accomplish that?**

A solution is relationship marketing. I recommend staying in touch by "relationship pinging," which I've have been doing for over 20 years. In *Never Eat Alone*, Keith Ferrazi calls a 'ping' - "a quick casual greeting." A reason this strategy is so effective is that people are starved for affection because with the advances of technology what is missing is connection. The results I have gotten from customized cards and gifts have been more effective at building and maintaining relationships than other methods such as email.

Here are eight referral and relationship building strategies that I use:

1. Shelf life - This builds relationships and keeps you top-of-mind. One of the best methods is to send a picture of you with your client. For women, the picture can be of you and her. For men, the picture should include his favorite toy, such as a boat or car.

Another benefit to the shelf life strategy is that others who see it will ask who is that person in that picture with you.

2. The birthday strategy - My favorite relationship pinging strategy is sending clients heartfelt cards for their birthday. For top clients, send a card and a gift and even take them to lunch. One of the best ways to acquire referrals is to have a "Birthday Breakfast" or "Birthday Lunch" for your client. Take a group picture of attendees which includes you, and then send it to all who went to the party as well as those who couldn't make it. Make sure that the message focuses on building and maintaining your relationship with the recipient and not your business.

3. The anniversary strategy - This is especially successful with women and married couples. Instead of sending a card on their anniversary, send an anniversary card on the day they began working with you. Include a picture of you and them on the front.

4. The holiday strategy - This consists of sending mailers, cards and postcards to prospects throughout the year.

- January: The New Year

- February: Valentine's Day. For women include truffles or goodies.

- March: St. Patrick's Day. Send an invitation to a St. Patrick's gathering. Ask everyone to bring their favorite food in green.

- April: Happy spring or Happy Easter.

- May: Memorial Day. This is very effective for retired veterans and their spouses.

- July: Independence Day, July 4.

- September: Labor Day.

- November: Thanksgiving. Add some humor or include a heartfelt message.

- December: Holiday card. Include a picture of your family; this is much more effective than sending a generic card!

5. The brownie strategy - Send a card and box of brownies and ask the person to call you when he/she receives it. This is one of the most effective strategies, with call-back rates as high as 80 percent. It also has our highest ROI for referral marketing.

6. Let's do lunch - This can be used to meet and cultivate centers of influence, prospects, clients and reciprocal referral partnerships. This strategy has gotten the best results from males, entrepreneurs and business owners.

With women, a group lunch works better. Inside the card include a message such as, "I enjoy meeting interesting people and would like to treat you to lunch." This strategy, if done correctly, generates up to 45 percent call-backs for a lunch appointment.

7. Who do you know - This technique requires a great referral card. On the inside of the card you can say, "I am expanding my business, and I'm looking for people just like you." On one side of it, you have your short letter of introduction; on the other flap, describe your ideal client.

8. Let's Share Referrals - This is the best strategy for reciprocal, referral relationship partnerships. The secret to this strategy is to set expectations with your referral partners.

The best relationship marketing pinging strategies include alternating among various methods. To be effective, the message needs to be all about them, not business. The referral marketing pinging should be soft and subtle. Prospects want an advisor with whom they have a deep relationship and one who will listen and help them solve their problems.

Annette Bau, CFP®

Founder of *MillionaireSeries.com* & *AdvisorMarketing Practices.com*

Email: info@MillionaireSeries.com

Website: MillionaireSeries.com

Annette is the founder of *MillionaireSeries.com* & *AdvisorMarketingPractices.com* to help advisors create their dream business and life. She is the author of four books and numerous best-selling products, including *The Million Dollar Marketing System* and *101 Insider Secrets for Marketing to Affluent Women.*

PART 3

How To Generate Quality Leads

Chapter 19

Marketing Long Term Care Insurance With Partnership

By Phyllis Shelton

Q. My state has a LTCI Partnership program. How can I use partnership as a way to generate leads?

Consider these facts:

- Today, Medicaid is the primary payer for America's long term care costs, a solution that is unsustainable.[1]

- Long term care makes up a third of state Medicaid budgets and is projected to grow to half by 2030.[2]

- This country has 80 million baby boomers facing their long term care years, and 95% of them have no coverage for long term care.[3]

- This dependency on Medicaid will worsen as new legislation goes into effect on January 1, 2014, that will add 16 million more people to the Medicaid rolls.[4]

- Health care reform is now expanding the Medicaid home care benefits for LTCI beginning in 2011, which will bring people out of the woodwork to claim these benefits.[5]

The solution is providing a public-private partnership insurance plan that allows the private sector to pay for LTCI first and makes Medicaid the payer of last resort. The four states that embraced this concept in the early 1990's proved it to be a home run. Of the approximately 325,000 people who purchased LTCI Partnership policies in Connecticut, New York, Indiana and California, less than 500 have had to turn to Medicaid after using their LTC insurance benefits first.[6] Not only does this program help state budgets, it provides the family with private-pay choices as long as possible.

So, how do you frame this conversation in your marketing efforts and use it to generate leads? Here are ideas to get the message out in your community.

- Book yourself on local talk radio stations by using this message: *"This is not just about private insurance. It's about delivering a service to the people. Caregiving robs individual freedom to work a full-time job, to send children to college or to take a vacation. People want to maintain their lifestyles and not to be a burden on their children."*

- Participate in seminars with attorneys, financial planners, CPAs and banks. Explain how clients can have unlimited Medicaid benefits if insurance isn't enough without spending down most of their assets. At the same time, they can remain independent as long as possible as private-pay patients. Some may prefer to remain a private-pay patient, but it's our job to explain the options.

- Write a series of articles for your clients or local publications that emphasize the impact of LTCI on the family (emotionally and financially), on employers, on the state and on the nation. Position Partnership LTCI plans as the solution to have private-pay dollars pay first and Medicaid last.

Use direct mail

If you are active with direct mail, try this message:

Heading
Dear_____ :

Congress has already put the seal of approval on long term care insurance (LTCI) by providing tax incentives to purchase these policies and by making it more difficult to qualify for Medicaid LTCI benefits. Now, Congress has approved another great incentive to help Americans pay for long term care!

An LTCI Partnership policy is available in our state that offers you dollar-for-dollar asset protection if you ever have to ask the government to help pay for your long term care. What does this mean? It means that instead of spending down to [$2,000]* if you need to apply for Medicaid LTCI benefits, you will be allowed to keep a dollar of assets for every dollar of LTCI insurance benefits you have received. For example, if your policy has paid $200,000 in benefits, you would be allowed to keep $202,000 of assets when you apply for Medicaid, and that much would also be exempt from estate recovery when you die.

It's legislation like this that makes it hard to ignore LTCI, an issue that has moved to center stage as more and more of us are caring for family members who need extended care. You will hear phrases like "the United States is in the midst of a significant and growing caregiving crisis."

Please return the enclosed postage-paid reply card to request a free booklet that provides additional information on the new partnership between Medicaid and LTC insurance and how recent health care reform affects LTCI financing.

Sincerely,

- Offer to do a training session for the Senior Health Insurance Program in your state. These are state employees who are expected to answer consumer questions about LTC insurance. They need and want training so they can do a better job, but in many states funds are too limited to provide paid training.

So many employees are interested in LTCI because of family experiences, but have no desire to shop for it. They wait for their employer to do the shopping as the employer has done for other benefits. Then they buy at all ages because they figure if it wasn't appropriate for their age group, the employer wouldn't be offering it to them!

Best of all, a down economy has heightened awareness of the importance of LTCI with employees. The Partnership's asset protection feature drives this point home with a "protect what you have left" message.

The fastest and easiest way to get leads through the Partnership is to network with health insurance agents and employee benefit advisors. They are being asked about LTCI by employers who are being asked about it by employees who are caregivers.

Cultivate all of these centers of influence by providing simple handouts with your contact information on it, and watch the leads come pouring in!

Phyllis Shelton

President of LTC Consultants
Phone: 615-590-0300
Email: info@ltcconsultants.com
Website: www.ltcconsultants.com
Phyllis is the founder of LTC Consultants, a company that has provided educational materials and training to the long term care insurance industry since 1991. An expert in the industry, she has written four books about LTC Insurance, including her most recent: *Protecting Your Family with Long-Term Care Insurance.*

Footnotes

1 "National Health Expenditures by Type of Service and Source of Funds for Calendar Years 2008 to 1960", Centers for Medicare and Medicaid Services, 1/10 and Eiken, Sredl, Burwell and Gold. "Medicaid LTC Expenditures in FY 2009", Thomson Reuters, 8/17/10;

2 "Medicaid Long-Term Care: The Ticking Time Bomb", Deloitte Center for Health Solutions, 6/21/10;

3 "Economic Downturn Impacting Women's Ability to Plan for Long-Term Care Costs, New Survey Finds", AHIP, 1/9/09;

4 Congressional Budget Office, "H.R. 4872, Reconciliation Act of 2010 (Final Health Care Legislation)", 3/20/10;

5 CMS HHS Letter to State Medicaid Directors, 8/6/10 re: Improving Access to Home and Community-Based Services, SMDL #10-015, ACA #6 http:// www.hhs.gov/od/topics/community/iathcbssmd8-6-102.pdf;

6 Reports from CT, NY, IN, CA LTC Partnership Directors as of 9/30/10.

Chapter 20

See More People: The Proven Method To Increase Business

By Bill Good

Q. *I need help with prospecting so I can get more qualified LTCI prospects in the pipeline. Can you provide some suggestions?*

It's an art to balance your prospecting and selling lives. But it's essential that you sustain your prospecting effort to see more people. One way is to set aside several hours a day to prospect. Based on where you are in your career, you have to decide how many hours you need to spend.

When you are brand new, prospect eight to ten hours a day. After a few weeks, you can't do that anymore because you now have prospects to follow up with. Once you have a prospecting pipeline in place, the most you should prospect is about three hours per day; the least is one hour per day.

Consider this block of time set aside for prospecting to be an appointment with yourself to create your future. Your goal should be to do something every day to generate new business; and on some days, do a lot. What are you going to do during the prospecting time block? You have three choices: 1) Pound the phones, and 2) Research people your clients may know, or 3) Get a mailing out the door.

If you're making phone calls, either to people who have not registered on the DNC or to seminar attendees, your usual best time is 8 a.m. to 10 a.m. If you have help, instruct your assistant to handle all incoming calls, unless it's a prospect who is returning a call. All other incoming calls should be noted as messages. Pick them up when you are done with your prospecting. If you don't have help, just send any incoming calls to voice mail. Don't break the momentum.

Make calling count

If you are going to be on the phone, make it count! Call for 50 minutes and take a ten minute break. During your break, get up, walk around, but keep your eye on a clock. After ten minutes, pick up the phone. Short, concentrated bursts of cold calling are, in my opinion, preferred over long, tiring days. If you are making cold calls, your goal should be 40 to 60 dials per hour. If you are calling back existing prospects, shoot for 20 to 40.

Suppose cold calling is not your cup of tea. A valid use of your prospecting time is to research people that your existing, and hopefully happy, clients know. Once you have identified someone, e.g. a next door neighbor, you can call an existing client and say, *"By the way, a couple of your neighbors are on one of my marketing lists. I was planning to give them a call, but wanted to check with you first. Do you know _____ and _____?"* Wait for his or her response and then say, *"When I talk with them, is it okay if I mention that you are one of my good clients/friends?"*

What about mailings? Get stationery and envelopes, and handwrite short notes to existing clients and prospects. Keep your name in front of the people you know. Otherwise, you will fade from memory.

Consider sending some government documents. Enter this exact set of characters into a Google search box: "long term care" site:*.gov filetype:pdf. You will be amazed at the free (and copyright-free) information you can get.

Bill Good
Bill Good Marketing, Inc.
Phone: 801-572-1480, ext 1291
Email: billgood@billgoodmarketing.com
Website: www.billgood.com
Bill is the author of *Hot Prospects*. He designs prospecting and client marketing campaigns, one of which has been running successfully for 25 years.

Chapter 21

Setting Appointments: Psychology Of The Phone

By Michael Dornfeld

Q. *I dread making phone calls. Some mornings I want to do anything except dial that phone to set appointments. How can I overcome that feeling?*

You must build time into your schedule to set appointments because that's how sales are generated. A lot of people have phone reluctance. This is where you know what you need to do, but you have a block that prevents you from picking up the phone and making calls. Some of us create negative thoughts in our head: the prospects will yell at me, they are not interested, I'm bothering them, and a whole host of other feelings.

It all comes down to the fear of rejection. Prospects are not rejecting you. They do not know you or forgot they inquired about LTC insurance. People are programmed to get you off the phone as quickly as possible, so they are not taken advantage of. Once you understand and accept this, it will make it easier for you to persevere. Here is my simple rule for the telephone: some will, some won't, so what. Someone else is waiting for your call. You need to believe that you're probably the only person who will ever have the chance to talk to prospects about this difficult subject. You have the answers to their problems. Maintain the attitude that they are very lucky to have you helping them with their LTC issues. Once your beliefs are in check and you are in congruence with the sales process, the dials are much easier to make.

Here's an exercise to put everything into perspective. Answer these questions: How many dials on average does it take for you to set an appointment? How many appointments does it take for you to make a sale? What is your average premium sold? What is your average placement rate? What is your annualized commission?

This will tell you how much money you are making per dial. How important would it be if you knew that on a 100 dials a week you set eight appointments? You ended up seeing six appointments. You closed three of them for $6,900 with a 70 percent placement rate, netting you $4,830. Your annualized commission would be $____ for the week. You made $____ from 100 dials which netted you $____ per dial. If you were paid $ ____ per dial, how many dials would you make every day? This is a business, and you need to keep track of your numbers, so you know if you are on target to reach your goals.

Your phone script needs to be conversational. In other words, you need to internalize it by writing it out by hand several times. This exercise will enable you to sound conversational, rather than sounding as if you're reading from a script. Once you are comfortable with this, you can put your own personality into the call and have fun. These simple steps allow you to build a rapport with the prospect that will translate into an appointment.

Health matters

Nearly one third of respondents who request information on LTCI are not eligible due to changes in their medical history. Here's the script I use to obtain answers about health history. *"Mr./Mrs._____, I don't want to waste your time so I need to ask you some health questions. Have either of you been hospitalized in the last five years?" Have you or your spouse had any of the following health issues?*

1. *A stroke, TIA or heart attack?*

2. *Cancer? If so, what stage cancer was it? What kind of treatment did you undergo? Did the cancer spread to the lymph nodes? How long since your last treatment?)*

3. *Diabetes? How is it controlled? If insulin, how many units? What is your most recent A1C results?*

4. *Hypertension? How often does your doctor monitor your blood pressure? What was your last reading? How long have you been medicated? Hypertension is a disease, and people do not put enough emphasis on*

this. Just because something is common, it can still be serious. The leading complications of hypertension disease are congestive heart failure, circulatory issues, heart attack and stroke.

5. *Heart or circulation problems?*

6. *Are you taking any prescription medications? If yes, what are they? What problems are they treating? What are the dosages?*

7. *Is your weight proportional to your height? If the prospects seem unsure, just ask what their height and weight were at their last doctor's visit?*

8. *Are there any other health issues, which you do not believe to be important, but that I need to be made aware of?*

If you find that the clients have had a big change in their medical histories, you can call the underwriting department for each carrier to see if they are willing to examine an application from these individuals.

What do you think is going through the clients' minds while they are waiting for you to get back to them? People want what they can't have, and they are hoping they still have a chance to get this coverage. If the underwriters tell you that they will look at an application, you can tell your client that there is only a small window of opportunity in which they can qualify for this type of coverage. In most cases, you will set the appointment.

Financially qualify

Ask the clients, *"Were you mainly looking at LTCI to protect your assets or so that you will not be a burden on others?"* Validate their answers, *"Good for you. Many of the people I speak with also say the same thing."* Next, say, *"Most people who are looking into this type of protection have assets excluding their home of $100,000 or more. Do you fit into that category?"* If they answer *"yes,"* add, *"Now I understand why you started looking into this."* If they say *"no,"* they may not be candidates for this coverage.

In response to your telephone call, some clients will say, *"I changed my mind." "Just mail me the information." "I'm not interested."* You can say the following to deflect their answers:

"Mr./Mrs. _____, most of the people I speak to feel the same way, until I remind them that when they returned the card/lead to my office, they had one of two concerns. The first concern was they didn't want to be a burden to their children. The second was that they didn't want to spend down their retirement portfolio. Which one of these was your concern when you returned the card/request to my office?"

Once the prospective clients commit to either concern, they have admitted that they are interested in LTCI. This answer may not work all of the time, but it opens the discussion and presents an opportunity for you to set an appointment.

Finally, say, *"Many people who have decided to address this issue have had some direct experience in which a family member required long term care. Does anyone in your immediate or extended family require home visits by a specialist or care in a facility now? Or perhaps in the past?"* If the answer is *"yes,"* then respond, *"Now I see why you're looking into this coverage."* If *"no,"* say, *"I'm glad to see that you are being proactive in order to protect your family."*

Setting the appointment

You need to market yourself on the telephone as someone who is in high demand. Do not respond in the following manner: *"Mr._____, I have an opening on Monday at 10 a.m. or would Tuesday at 7 p.m. be better"?* The client says "No." You say, *"OK. How about Monday at 1 p.m. or Tuesday at 4 p.m.?"* Again, the client says, "No." You say, *"How about Wednesday at 7 p.m. or Thursday at 10 a.m.?"* Does this sound like someone who is professional and whose services are in demand? Indeed not! This sounds like someone who is desperate for an appointment.

Even if you have no appointments on your calendar, you must market yourself as if you have very few openings. You can accomplish this by telling the prospect that your calendar is booked for the rest of the week, but you have some availability the following week. Ask the clients to check their calendars, so that you can find a mutually convenient time. You can tell your prospects that you can give them about an hour of your time, as you have many people who are interested in this insurance.

Michael Dornfeld

Since 1996, Michael has held many positions in the LTC insurance industry that contributed to the growth and distribution of Long Term Care insurance sales.

Chapter 22

How To Efficiently Track And Organize Prospects

By Larry Weigel

Q. I want to track and organize qualified prospects on a consistent basis. Can you suggest a system to accomplish that?

An efficient system for prospecting will result in more qualified prospects on a consistent basis. I use a self-assessment tool, which I call calculating your PSAT score.

This assessment score reflects how well you, the professional, do the following tasks:

- **P** Prospecting or prequalifying

- **S** Sales: who, where, what and how

- **A** Achievement: purpose, passion and money

- **T** Tracking: list, code, how often, follow -up and sorting

To determine the score, assess yourself on each statement below. A score of 0 = worst, and 10 = best. Total the score. The maximum is 100 percent.

I have identified traits for my ideal client which will help ensure that he/she is qualified for LTCI. I use these criteria when I meet with a prospect.

1. I have set a minimum compensation amount that I am willing to accept before I agree to work with a prospect or client.

2. I block out time each week to schedule sales appointments.

3. I keep cumulative statistics on sales results and set specific sales goals each year.

4. I know the amount of commission income from renewals that I receive from each client.

5. In my work, I am driven more by purpose than money.

6. I have an alphabetical list of all my clients and prospect accounts.

7. I have established designation levels for each client in order to determine the frequency of contacts.

8. I have a follow-up ticker system that I use each month to identify clients and prospects who have agreed to meet at a future date.

9. I can sort each name in my client file by prospect, client, product sold, pending business status, claims, etc.

As a multi-line producer, I learned it is important to leverage my time well while maximizing client communications. I can only provide services to, and maintain ongoing communication with, a finite number of clients. To facilitate this process, I assign a contact code to each individual. That code designates a specific category that reflects the level of attention required for each.

Level 1 - People who do not receive regular, on-going communication from me. Of my 650 client accounts, 50 percent fall in this category.

Level 2 - Planning Trail. These people have indicated that in addition to LTCI, they want to know more about other services the firm offers such as life insurance and retirement planning. Twenty-five percent are in this group. Using Excel, I code each person "contact at a specific date in the future."

Level 3 - VIP. I will maintain regular annual contact with this individual. Examples include possible referral sources and centers of influence. Another 25 percent fall into this group which represents my best referral base because these people fit my ideal client profile.

The "Right Fit" client profile for individuals:

- Married

- Empty nesters, 55-65 years of age

- Net income $50,000, plus liquid assets of $250,000 or more, not counting the home.

I invite individuals who fit this profile to client appreciation events and I maintain on-going contact through such communication tools as cards and newsletters.

The "Right Fit" client profile for corporate clients:

- Owners of closely held businesses, which have 50 employees or less, and are profitable.

- Ideally the business holds C-corporation tax status because of the opportunity for individual executive carve-out options and full deductibility of costs through the company. C-corporation status offers the best opportunity for prospects.

- To a lesser degree, businesses which hold S-Corporation status.

- To a lesser degree, businesses run by sole proprietor.

By using contact codes, I have created a built-in prospecting tool and a list of suitable people to call for appointments. This allows me to focus on what I should be doing each day.

Larry Weigel, CLTC

Medical Risk Management Specialist for Keating and Associates, a financial planning group.

Phone: 785-537-0366

Email: larryw@keatinginc.com

Website: www.themedicarecoach.com

Larry is the creator of the national Medicare Coach program which provides fee based "coaching" to seniors so that they can make informed choices on what products work best for them based on their individual needs.

Chapter 23

Generating Ink:
A Public Relations Primer
For LTCI Producers

By Jesse Slome

Q. *If I can become the LTCI expert quoted in my local newspaper, I can share the reprinted article with clients, prospects and centers of influence. How can I make this happen?*

Public relations is a powerful communications tool that is highly effective in creating an image for you and your business. Being quoted in the media is a smart way to market yourself.

Here are the simple steps to start making yourself a personal publicity machine:

1. Know how to create an effective news release - A news release or a press release is still an effective tool to generate local publicity. However, media outlets receive hundreds of them daily. So how do you write one that will grab the media's attention and make them see why it's important to print your news item or to call you for more information?

Your press release must catch the eye of the reader. The headline is the most important element of your press release, and it should be carefully considered. Generally, there are two types of headlines, depending on the subject matter of your release. The "newsworthy headline" can be used if the information has a hard news angle, for example, "LTCI Associates Appoints New President."

Other times, a more creative approach is warranted because you want the headline to capture the interest of the reader. Be careful, however, to avoid jargon or make the headline so obscure that it isn't clear to a layman. Here's an example of a creative headline, "Women Unaware Of Significant Ways To Save On Long Term Care Insurance."

The next part of your press release is the lead, or the first sentence or paragraph. Your lead must draw in the reader. The reader of your lead, typically the editor, should know the answer to the following two questions: What's happening? and Why should I care? Simply, your lead tells them why the information is important, why it's important to their readers and, the most essential, why they want to read on.

To compare, here are two leads that convey the same information in a very different manner. Which would make you, as the editor, choose to read on?

Version 1 - Sarah Jones, a leading long term care insurance professional with ABC Insurance Agency in Chattanooga, will host a free seminar next Tuesday on what women need to know about long term care planning.

Version 2 - Women are three times more likely to need long-term care than men. A special free planning seminar for women will take place next Tuesday featuring one of Chattanooga's leading long term care planning experts.

Now that you have the recipient reading, you need to provide the supporting information and details. Provide the most important information first and work your way down to the least important details. If you offer facts, cite the source. You want the editor to understand what kind of story he/she can pursue with this information. Don't overload the editor with too much information.

Your press release should be one or at most two pages printed on plain white paper without letterhead. Most important, it must contain information on whom to contact for further information. Generally, this is done at the very top of the first page.

For More Information, contact:
(name)
(phone)
(email)

Include your cell phone number. To make it clear that you're a local professional, use your local phone number. To further reinforce this point, include your address.

There are commonly accepted standards for a press release. Readability and impact are what you are after, and thus I recommend you start with a very bold, enlarged headline. Use two lines for your headline if necessary. The body copy of your news release should be double spaced with a clear, readable font. Arial 12 point works well.

If you're having difficulty coming up with newsworthy ideas for press releases, you can use the services of companies that sell ghostwritten press releases and articles. Just add your personal information and distribute it to local media in your area.

2. Know what's newsworthy - Which of the following would you consider newsworthy?

- IRS Announces Increased Tax Deductibility Limits For Long Term Care Insurance

- Free Estate Planning Seminar Scheduled

- Free Booklet Explains Ways To Save On Long Term Care Insurance

All three are newsworthy. Tax law changes and new limits are always of interest to business editors. A free seminar featuring local experts is perfect for the Community Calendar section. And, every editor likes to tell his/her readers about free items. That's why literally every public relations agency creates some sort of free guide it can publicize. Best of all, offering something free is about the only way you can get your phone number included as part of an editorial article. Want prospects? Offer a free booklet; there are many that focus on LTCI information and insurance.

Other reasons to send a press release that will get published include:

- Earning a designation

- Joining a prestigious professional organization

- Receiving an award or recognition

- Speaking at an event

- Sponsoring of a charity event

- Conducting a local survey, e.g., cost of care in your city compared to national averages

- Offering a free booklet

3. Identifying the right people - If you hired a public relations professional, do you know how he/she would find out to whom to send press releases? The professional might know an editor or two, but for the most part, he/she would pick up the phone and cold call editors. That's what you are going to need to do as well.

Before you call anyone, review the pages of your local daily newspaper every day for a week. Look for possible places where your story could appear. Does this paper publish a calendar of local events? That's perfect for seminars you might hold. Does it have a "Seniors" editor? That's someone you certainly want to send information. Each newspaper will identify the names of writers as well as have a box that contains the media outlet's contact information.

Look for local contacts. For example, your paper may run items from syndicated columnists or wire services. These are not the folks you want. Your local community weekly newspaper will have an editor. Your local daily newspaper will have a Business Editor. Those are the people you want to contact.

Finally, go to the local library or supermarket. You will find stacks of free publications, some of which you may not know existed. Maybe it's a business journal produced by the local Chamber of Commerce or a free newspaper that targets seniors or parents. Take one, and find the contact information for the local editor.

Now you're ready to pick up the phone. Try to call mid-week, Tuesday or Wednesday, in the morning. Here's a script that you might use:

"Good morning, Mr. Jones. My name is Mary Smith, and I'm a local long term care insurance professional located here in Austin. I'm calling because as I meet with area folks, I see there's so much they don't know about long term care planning, or worse are mistaken about. That's why I'd like to get you some relevant information about the topic

and send you my card in case you're ever writing about the topic. What's the best way to send you information?"

Ask how he/she prefers to receive information. Mail still works and be sure to obtain the correct mailing address. However, most editors will also favor email. My suggestion is that you do both. Today, many people work from home or off-site locations. You want them to see your press release and not have an administrative person open it.

Now you've opened the door, from there it's relationship building. I always like to ask editors how old they are. Someone who is 50 likely has aging parents who may be dealing with LTCI, while someone age 35 has no clue what we're talking about.

After that initial call, mail a very short thank you letter and paperclip your business card. If your card doesn't specifically mention LTCI, write "Long Term Care Planning" on the card in red ink. Your goal is that the editor will save your name for when he/she needs information or a comment.

4. Sending your press releases - When mailing, looking local is a good thing because editors are most concerned about their local constituents. The envelope should have your return address printed clearly on the front. Use a postage stamp, not a meter. Your mailing will appear more personal, and the cancellation reinforces the local flavor.

Here's a final word of advice. Publicity is sales. Sometimes the client, who in this case is the editor, buys at the first appointment. Sometimes it takes multiple contacts.

Don't give up. If you make the commitment to create and send press releases, if you provide editors with truly newsworthy information and if you keep positioning yourself as the local expert, your name will appear in your local newspaper as a LTCI professional.

Jesse Slome

Executive Director, American Association for Long-Term Care Insurance
Phone: 818-597-3227
Email: jslome@aaltci.org
Website: www.aaltci.org
Jesse is the executive director of the American Association for Long-Term Care Insurance. AALTCI is responsible for creating Long-Term Care Awareness Month. He is an award-winning marketing and public relations professional who has worked for leading national public relations agencies.

Chapter 24

How To Use Radio To Create LTC Awareness
By Phil Grossman

Q. *I've been approached by a local radio station to advertise. Does this medium generate leads?*

I have been marketing only long term care insurance since 1997. For my first six years, I taught two seminars every month. I would advertise these seminars in three local newspapers. I worked these seminars to increase name recognition, exposure, brand imaging and experience. In addition, I took out newspaper ads in local papers, homeowners' association telephone books, the Yellow Pages, and church and temple newsletters. I became a "lead junkie," but due to my multiple marketing efforts, I did generate a considerable amount of premium.

The second half of my LTCI marketing life is dramatically different from the first half. I have eliminated all print advertising except for one monthly local publication. I work exclusively through referrals from certified financial planners and other financial professionals. I do not purchase leads or teach seminars any longer. My entire advertising budget is spent on radio.

Radio advertising works! Each week, I purchase eighteen 60 second radio spots. These are spread over seven days, Monday though Friday, concentrating in the 7 a.m. to 5 p.m. time slots on the Financial Talk News radio station. These commercials brand Phil Grossman, Long Term Care Specialist.

I do not discuss prices, benefits or companies. I provide 60 seconds of information and education 18 times a week. I have been doing this since April, 2009. As part of this advertising campaign, I also participate in a "Financial Fair" sponsored by the radio station. My participation involves manning a 10x10 exhibit booth and a personally hosted seminar for 45 people. In 2009, over 2200 people attended the fair. The majority of these individuals have heard my advertising. At that fair, I received over 200 inquiries and wrote 15 applications.

I have recorded six different advertisements to air on the radio, and I rotate these with the hope that listeners will not tune me out. Although the recent economy has reduced my responses, I remain very happy with my results. I still see radio as the most immediate vehicle to generate a sale, and I will continue to do this until the environment changes.

—

Phil Grossman

President and CEO of Long Term Care Options, Inc.
Phone: 602-531-2200
Email: ltcoptions@gmail.com
Website: www.ltcpro4u.com
Specializing exclusively in long term care planning since 1997, Phil is the top producer in Arizona and ranked 15th nationally.

Chapter 25

The Elevator Speech – Openings To Help Close The Sale

By Ron Hagelman

Q. *Can you suggest some effective phrases that will grab peoples' attention and get them interested in looking at LTC insurance?*

As I view the LTCI sale, there are really only two reasons consumers sign that first check: 1) They are the kind of folks whom we have always helped leverage risk: those who think ahead, plan ahead and, frankly, care ahead; and 2) those who have been touched by an angel, meaning they have directly experienced the emotional and financial firestorm that a caregiving event can be.

To reach the rest of the people, the vast majority of LTC prospects, one needs a conversation, a direct and succinct verbal assault that is insightful, thought provoking and nonthreatening. That is the way to open and close the sale.

There is a legend in our business of the agent who made the Million Dollar Round Table just by riding an elevator in a large office building. He had only a few minutes to make his points, provide assistance, drive home the necessity to take action and then ask for an opportunity to elaborate.

Now, what does one say to connect to these potential sales? First, ask over and over again, "Do you have your LTCI protection yet?" This question should be followed immediately by an explanation of why you purchased your own policy.

Every planning conversation must include the identification and examination of retirement dollars. The most direct, and perhaps most powerful, explanation of what LTCI accomplishes is retirement security. You must dispel the notion that the sale is about the insured. Instead, it's about the family and loved ones who will surround the claim.

You must end both the lie that somehow LTCI is an optional expense and the perception that leveraging the LTCI risk is somehow a financial planning variable. There is no choice. Families benefit when individuals take action to protect themselves through the purchase of LTCI.

As an insurance professional, you have an ongoing responsibility to speak firmly of the inevitable nature of the risk. The inescapable truth is you will get older, your health will change and you will need care. Care is very expensive, and it will be even more expensive when you need it.

For those potential clients who are by nature more analytical, start by operating on the assumption that you would not even presume to sell LTCI to others if you did not already own your own policy. Tell them, *"You know I had a $1,000,000 problem. Do you share my problem?"* Explain the current annual cost, current typical claim duration and the degree to which inflation impacts costs 30 years in the future. Now ask the obvious, *"Where will the money come from? Where is your million dollars?"* It is very very simple. This bill will not go away. Someone must pay it. Will you pay it through insurance or will the government pay for you when you become a welfare recipient?

Seeking the caregiving connection

A favorite way of reaching the client is to seek the caregiver connection. Ask these probing outcome questions, "Who will care for you? Whose life have you chosen to disrupt? Which family member will lift you, dress you, bathe you and change you?" A conversation about the changes in the current law may offer an entry. "Did you know that the law has changed and your assets are now at risk?" Discuss the Deficit Reduction Act (DEFRA) of 2005, explaining the change in transfer of assets regulations. Prior to DEFRA, the look-back period for the transfer of assets was three years from the date of transfer. Now it is five years from the date of Medicaid eligibility. Today, it is extremely difficult to hide your money.

Most people are not aware of the benefits of partnership plan ownership. Here is an excellent opportunity to tap into resentment of government sponsored asset recovery. Ask, *"Are you aware you can now protect your chosen assets from estate recovery? I'm sure you don't want the state to sell your home to pay your Medicaid bill."* A partnership sale is very straightforward. *"Who is it in your life that you care enough about to protect from the state? Is there any part of your legacy that you wish to leave to your children and grandchildren?"*

I have other favorite openings. The Pension Protection Act and the availability of favorably priced and underwritten combination life and annuity products lead directly to these questions. *"Does your life or annuity policy pay for long term care if needed? If I could protect your assets and dramatically increase your benefit values for long term care, would you be willing to listen?"* In addition, now that you can 1035 LTCI and help to improve the customer's risk position, you don't even have to ask for new money. This is the perfect opportunity for a policy review.

Today's core question focuses on the booming multi-life small group market. If someone is actively at work, you no longer have to apologize that you cannot provide protection. Based on recently lowered requirements for the number of lives needed to provide modified guarantee issue underwriting, the hottest new question when you uncover an underwriting problem becomes, *"Where do you work?"* With a sufficient number of lives, almost everyone regardless of underwriting status may be eligible for LTCI coverage!

—

Ron Hagelman

President, Republic Marketing Group
Phone: 888-620-4066
Email: ron@rmgltci.com
Website: www.rmgltci.com
Ron is a nationally recognized motivational speaker and monthly LTCI columnist for Broker World magazine. He also serves as a Master Trainer for the LTCP designation and has been a member of the LIMRA and SOA LTCI Committees. Ron is currently president of "America's Long Term Care Insurance Experts" a national network of brokerage general agencies specializing in LTCI sales and marketing.

Chapter 26

Developing An Effective Elevator Pitch

By Suzanne Bates

Q. *I'm focusing on doing more networking, so I need to develop an effective elevator pitch. Could you provide some guidelines about what I should say when meeting new people?*

How many times have you asked someone at a networking event what they do for a living, only to regret it? You find yourself trapped by a person who has taken your question as an invitation to deliver a long, detailed elevator pitch.

In the "old days" before we were coached to prepare these elevator pitches, we used to say, *"I'm an accountant,"* or *"I have a law practice."* It wasn't clever, but it did the job. If the person was interested in learning more, they would ask.

It's time to reexamine the purpose of the pitch and talk about when it's even appropriate.

Let's start with the big myth – you don't have 30 seconds. You might have 10 or 12. When you start a conversation and someone asks what you do for a living, make it a conversation. Say something brief and interesting about what you do.

Once you state what you do, ask the other person a question. They won't be interested in you until you're interested in them. The way to express interest is by trying to actually learn something about them and by finding common ground. Once you have made a genuine connection, the conversation will flow naturally; and they will probably ask about your business as well.

There are times when you must be prepared to stand up and give a little pitch about what you do. At many networking events, the meeting leader asks people to describe their business.

Even then, proceed with caution. Your pitch should be less than 30 seconds, and should be relevant to the audience and the event. Think of these venues as mini-presentations. The first rule of all public speaking applies. It's not about you. It's about them. It will be more memorable and interesting if what you say includes your audience.

Let me give you a great example. My book agent, Ken Lizotte, was attending a meeting of the Society for Professional Consultants. The host asked each person to stand and explain what kind of consulting they do.

Ken was racking his brain to come up with something relevant to this particular group. When his turn came, it finally came to him. He stood up and said, *"Hi. I'm Ken Lizotte, and I make people famous."* That got their attention! *"I do this by getting clients published in magazines and newspapers, and helping them get their books published, too."* After the meeting, he was immediately surrounded by a crowd of keenly interested people.

How can you apply this lesson to your elevator pitch? First, realize it isn't easy to make it simple. You have to analyze what you do for people, and boil it down to something interesting, concrete and about them.

- "Our company has a new drug that helps people sleep without the usual side effects."

- "I'm a political speechwriter working primarily with women running for national office."

- "Our firm works with family business owners looking for exit strategies."

If the other person expresses interest, you can follow up to explain how you do your work. Provide a couple of tangible, memorable phrases about how your product or service works. Leave the jargon at the office. That's a big turnoff, even in business conversation. Remember, you don't have to speak for three minutes; even 30 seconds works if your message is relevant and on the mark.

Here are a few general tips:

- Make it succinct and clear
- Create a word picture
- Make it concrete and simple
- Don't try to be overly clever
- Talk about results of your service or product
- Don't talk about yourself unless people ask
- Make the description inclusive – not too specific at first, so as not to eliminate potential customers or clients

Remember that you may need a variety of elevator pitches depending upon the audience.

It's always a good idea to try out your new pitches on people who know you and understand what you do. Make sure they are friends who will be honest. Don't accept "that sounds fine." Work on it until it feels right, you are comfortable saying it and it makes sense to a seventh grader.

If you feel anxious about delivering an elevator pitch - practice out loud. Get a tape recorder to practice, and do it until you can say it in your sleep. Keep refining – not lengthening. Make it short and interesting, and people will want to know more.

Suzanne Bates, CSP

CEO, Bates Communications, Inc.

Phone: 800-908-8239

Email: questions@bates-communications.com

Website: www.bates-communications.com

Bates Communication transforms leaders into powerful communicators who get business results. The firm offers strategic communications consulting, executive coaching, workshops and keynote speeches. Suzanne is the author of three books.

Chapter 27

How To Market To Associations

By Brian Johnson

Q. *I'm hearing that marketing to associations is a really good way to generate sales. Can you provide suggestions about how to be successful in this market?*

Association marketing instantly opens you up to a large group of qualified prospects to market to. In a sense, it's like going in the back door. If you want to work with physicians, then research the professional associations or societies they belong to, rather than trying to market directly to them. If you get an endorsement or sponsorship from a professional association, you're invited into the inner circle. You'll have the ability to attend the conferences, business meetings or any other activities the group organizes.

When an association or professional society sponsors or endorses a benefit, the members immediately trust the source, as it's already prescreened. You are no longer viewed as an insurance agent, but as a resource for information on a very important topic. In addition, association members are typically "planners" by nature, in that they see the value of investing in membership dues to further their personal or professional development. This is the type of client that purchases LTC insurance.

If the group has bylaws and the members pay dues, most insurance companies will extend a five to ten percent premium discount. The opportunities are endless - in 2004, it was estimated that there were 1.8 million associations in our country. And, if members are business owners and/or executives, this is a great door opener to multi-life cases.

In working with the Executive Director or the person who handles member benefits, emphasize the following key points:

- Associations need to bring ancillary benefits to the table that their members want in order to stay competitive.

- LTC planning is a hot topic, and a discount on a benefit that is perceived as expensive helps them attract and retain members.

- Zero cost to offer a discounted plan.

- Minimal administration.

- Demonstrates that the association cares about their members and their families.

- Sets them apart from those that do not offer this benefit.

- Saves members' time.

- Associations can earn non-dues revenue, since you as the agent will probably be advertising in their newsletters, attending trade shows, etc.

Your marketing efforts should piggyback the current communication methods that the association uses, such as email, hard copy newsletters and direct mail. You should have a presence across all communication channels. Do newsletter articles and a separate mailing about this new benefit - have your mailing approved by the association. Offer to speak at conferences. It's important to co-brand yourself with the association.

The best place to find associations and societies is from your current clients. Ask what groups they belong to and get the contact information. This way, you can call the executive director and explain that one of their members is your client and you would like to discuss how the Association could offer a discounted LTC insurance benefit at no cost for the group.

Additionally, consider the people you do business with – for example, your CPA, dentist and pharmacist. They all belong to a professional group. Or use the Internet and search for county and state associations.

Brian Johnson, MBA, CLTC

Director, Business Development, Affinity, Multi-Life and Group Long Term Care for National Long-Term Care Brokers, LLC

Phone: 800-695-8224, ext 154

Email: bjohnson@nyltcb.com

Website: www.nltcb.com

Brian coordinates with banks, credit unions, estate planning attorneys and CPA's to allow their clients to achieve a full integration of the core disciplines involved in effective estate and business planning. In addition, he manages affinity insurance discount programs for 13 professional associations and labor unions.

PART 4

The Client Presentation

Chapter 28

How To Explain The Risk Of Needing LTC In The Future

By Phil Grossman

Q. *I'm looking for an effective way to compare the LTCI risk with other risks that are commonly covered by insurance.*

I like to compare LTC to other areas where consumers have protected themselves by sharing the risk with an insurance company. These include homeowner's insurance (or renter's insurance), auto insurance and medical insurance. This comparison to other protection products helps illustrate to prospects that LTC is potentially the greatest risk they may face and it shouldn't be treated differently than the other three. I also use a visual to better explain the risk.

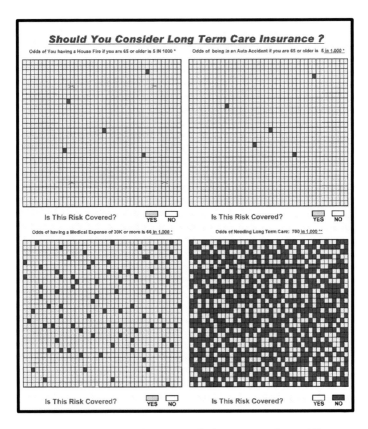

I start by explaining that LTCI is insurance that will cover you in the event you experience a major health event requiring long term care. I discuss their history of experiencing these events. I show them charts and explain that the charts illustrate industry figures reflecting the probability of these events happening. Most people have already purchased other types of insurance to protect against loss and hope they will never use them.

The first is insurance on your home. I ask prospects if they have ever filed a claim on their policy because of a fire. Most people will say never. I ask, *"How long have you had a home?"* The client will reply 10, 20, 50 years. I repeat back to them, *"So what you are saying is that in X number of years, you have never filed a claim for a fire on your home?"* Then I ask, *"Did you cancel your homeowner's insurance? You have not used it in X number of years, so I assume that you have come to the conclusion that it is a waste of money."* Why hasn't the client cancelled this coverage? The answer is that the client will always feel that there is a need for home insurance because you can never be sure what will happen in the future.

I show them the first chart, which illustrates that one out of 1000 will experience a claim on their homeowner's insurance for a fire. I explain the reason you have this protection is for peace of mind

The next question I ask pertains to the odds of their car being totaled, and then I ask if they have ever totaled a car. I structure my conversation similarly to the homeowner's insurance discussion. The risk is five in 1,000 (chart no. 2). I use the same approach for the third risk – the odds of a large hospital bill, which are 66 in 1,000 (chart no. 3).

I saved his life

At this point, I tell a story about living a life of significance. During a radio show that I appear on, a gentleman called to discuss LTCI. We made an appointment, and I went out to his home to meet with him and his wife. They were both in their 70s. She had considerable health issues, and I was quite concerned about her insurability.

When I pre-qualified him, he answered *"no"* to almost every question that is printed on an application. *"When was the last time you saw a doctor for any reason?"* I asked. He replied, *"It was several years ago."* He hadn't felt any need to see a doctor in all that time.

After a paramedical exam for underwriting, his Prostate-Specific Antigen level (PSA) was 37. He was treated for prostate cancer, and his PSA level dropped to less than 1. He now owns LTC insurance. My client believes that I may have saved his life. I do too.

The fourth risk is the probability of needing LTC. The risk for this is 700 out of 1000 or seven out of 10 (chart no. 4). I ask if the client has flown on commercial airline flights. If he or she answers yes, I then ask if there was a sign above the gangway to the plane that read, *"Passenger alert: Please be aware there is a 70% chance this flight will crash, would you get on the plane?"* I am trying to determine their risk tolerance as well as establish that this percentage only means something if we believe it applies to us! I continue comparing the flight risk I discussed with the probability that someone may need long term care. This has proven to be a very powerful tool that opens a client's eyes to the risk of needing LTC.

I close with asking, *"Is there any reason why you would not take care of the long term care risk in the same way you have taken care of the other three?"*

If they don't agree, I ask, *"Why would you ignore the one with the greatest risk and spend money on the less likely events? What you are saying is that you don't think it could happen to you."*

Their decision will be based on education, information and their belief that if you own property, you insure it. If I can't get a positive response to this comparison of risks, I then conclude the appointment and state that I cannot really help them. If they ask for price, I reply that if you don't feel you need or want it, price is irrelevant. Would you buy boat insurance at any price before you bought a boat?

Phil Grossman
President and CEO of Long Term Care Options, Inc.
Phone: 602-531-2200
Email: ltcoptions@gmail.com
Website: www.ltcpro4u.com
Specializing exclusively in Long Term Care Planning since 1997, Phil is the top producer in Arizona and ranked 15th nationally.

Chapter 29

How To Sell To The Wealthy? Don't Sell Product, Sell Advice.

By Harley Gordon

Q. *What key points should I make to convince my wealthy clients to purchase LTC insurance?*

First and perhaps most important you need to think about how you will be perceived by your client during the interview. If the focus of the conversation is on the risk of needing care and its consequences such as loss of independence, not being able to choose where your care is given and spending huge sums on it and then position LTCI as a solution, there is little doubt you will be viewed as a sales person trying to sell a product. That's because you have created an immediate mismatch of interests.

A mismatch of interests exists when you go into a meeting assuming that the client[1] is interested in what you have to say. If you are dealing with clients who have no prior experience, there is little doubt they are not interested in the above because they believe care will never be needed. Persisting in using statistics and, worse, educating the client about what care costs creates a selling environment: The client concludes you are not trying to educate him or her about something that is important to the client because you never asked, but rather are simply trying to sell a product he or she sees no need for.

The end result when working with the wealthy? The individual will simply tell you he or she has enough to cover the cost.

The five steps to success

Step 1 - Position yourself not as a presenter of product but as a professional in a field of study that has an impact on things and others that are important to the client. The field is extended care planning and the serious consequences providing care has on the wellbeing of those the client cares deeply about. The process starts with asking the simple but powerful question, *"What's important to you?"* People will insure things and others who are important to them. Once you know what and who they are, you can move to Step 2.

---

[1]Do not think of individuals as prospects but rather clients. The former are people you sell to things; the sale tends to focus on product and therefore transactional. The latter are those you sell advice to and therefore hold the potential for future business.

Step 2 - Educate the client about the two sets of consequences providing care has on those he (or she) loves. The first set is to their emotional and physical wellbeing. The second is to the financial viability of the family because paying for care causes a reallocation of income and assets, thereby compromising the client's ability to keep financial promises. It is important that at all times the focus be on what will happen to those he loves. Doing so compels the client to think about the consequences not having a plan and funding it properly would have on others. Once educated, it is likely the client will suggest that those consequences are unacceptable.

Step 3 - Don't offer LTCI as a solution but rather as a plan to mitigate the consequences you just set out. There are two reasons to do so:

1. The meeting has been based, not on trying to sell a product, but to educate the client about the consequences of providing care. Immediately shifting to product upsets the balance between trying to connect based on professionalism and wanting to conclude a sale. If you mention product at this stage, the client may conclude that your previous efforts were simply a ruse to sell it.

2. By allowing you to create a plan to protect his or her family you now have the right to ask, *"What do you think will fund it?"*

Step 4 - Funding the plan. Now that the plan is in place LTCI is positioned as the only viable funding source. That said, there is the issue of overcoming the objection of self-funding by those who truly do have enough assets to pay for care.

The traditional school of thought is to set out a case for spending huge amounts on care possibly bankrupting the family. This is counter-productive for two reasons: it is highly unlikely that a wealthy client (defined as those with at least $1,000,000 in investments) will spend all of it for care; only two carriers have paid one claim over this amount. Second, the client and his or her advisor are now convinced that your objective in the first place was to sell LTCI.

The better way to approach the subject is to remind the client and his or her advisor that assets do not pay for care; income does. Explain that you believe that a retirement portfolio should be looked at as capital in nature; capital assets are those that have the specific purpose of generating income. Therefore…

- $1,000,000 should not be looked at as paying for care, but rather as generating income in the vicinity of $40,000 per year.

- $2,000,000 should not be looked at as paying for care, but rather as generating income in the vicinity of $80,000 per year.

- $3,000,000 should not be looked at as paying for care, but rather as generating income in the vicinity of $120,000 per year.

As is the case with most successful clients, that income is likely committed to expenses few if any of which are discretionary. The client and advisor will have no choice but to agree. Continue by explaining that paying for care causes a reallocation of that income, thereby disrupting the client's ability to keep those financial commitments. If the response is that the client will simply use assets if care is needed, suggest that doing so will disrupt a plan to minimize taxes, wait out a down market and, perhaps most of all, impact the ability to continue generating income.

Harley Gordon

President, Corporation for Long-term Care Certification
Phone: 617-796-9788
Email: hgordon-1@ltc-cltc.com
Website: www.ltc-cltc.com
Attorney Harley Gordon is the principal creator of the CLTC designation. The program focuses on educating professionals how to create and properly fund a plan for extended care. Mr. Gordon's views have been featured on the PBS documentary *FrontLine*, *Wall Street Journal*, *National Underwriter*, *Senior Market Advisor* and the CBS News.

Chapter 30

Tips For Creating A Great Client Relationship

By Phil Grossman

Q. *I want to make my clients feel special and appreciated. How can I accomplish this during the sales process?*

I believe strongly in making sure that my prospects and clients know that I really care about them and that they feel comfortable working with me. In the many years I have been selling this protection, I have developed a number of effective techniques. Here are my suggestions:

- I always wear a badge showing my name, title and company. I find that it creates a level of comfort when the prospect can look through the window of their home and see who is there. Individuals are put at ease knowing that the person ringing their doorbell will be outside the door wearing a name badge. I've also had people stop me in the mall and grocery store and ask for more information.

- Before the appointment, I send the prospect a confirmation letter.

- I estimate that each home appointment will take 1 1/2 hours. If I am taking an application, I allow two hours.

- I always begin each interview with: "Why have you agreed to meet with me today?" and "Why do you think you might need long term care insurance?"

- A key phrase I frequently use is, *"You are an adult. I'm here to provide you with education and information. Then, you can decide if this coverage is appropriate and affordable for you."*

- Need, urgency and acceptable health are the key ingredients for a sale. I am there to help people address a challenging life experience they may have. You must represent yourself as a specialist and not someone who is looking for a sale. While respecting clients' privacy, you can tell stories about other situations you have encountered along with your own caregiving experiences. Be sincere.

- I call all my clients on their birthdays, even if I am out of town. I know their spouses' names and other important information, which I store in my PDA. All my files are also stored there so that important information is with me all the time.

- I ask for referrals when I deliver the policy. I say, "If you agree that this is something that is important, and I would assume that you do since you have decided to apply for coverage, I would like to have a couple of names of people whom you care about. If something would happen to them, then you could feel comfortable that at least you told them about this protection. Give them the opportunity to make the decision themselves."

- When asked about the cost, I respond, *"Have you ever eaten at a cafeteria? You go down the line, putting various items on the plate, and then you have to pay for it. That's like LTCI. The final price is based on what you decide to put on your plate".*

- *"If I give you a ballpark number, you would make a decision based on the number I give you. But that could be unfair to both you and me. What we need to have is a brief face-to-face discussion so that we can exchange some information and come up with a price that coordinates with a plan."*

In answer to the comment, just give me a rough idea, I reply as follows: *"I can't. If you call a dentist and say, 'I have a toothache.' and then ask 'How much will it cost?' the dentist won't know. I'm not a doctor, but we need to do an examination as well."*

- Within 24 hours after the home appointment, I send the applicant a thank you letter.

- For client application follow-ups, I have developed a method for keeping in touch. When I return from taking an application, I address three envelopes with the new client's information. I then put them into a file box with numbers from 1 to 31, corresponding to the days of the month. I insert the first envelope into the date two weeks from the application date. I insert the second envelope into the date in four weeks from the application. For the third, I insert it six weeks from the date of the application. Generally, a decision will have been made by that time.

The purpose of these envelopes is to ensure regular contact with clients and to inform them of their application status. When the policy is approved, I call and ask them if they have been getting my notes and whether they are happy with the process and the way they have been handled. I congratulate them that their application has been approved as we submitted it and explain that I should receive it within a week. When I receive it, I call to arrange delivery.

***

Phil Grossman

President and CEO of Long Term Care Options, Inc.
Phone: 602-531-2200
Email: ltcoptions@gmail.com
Website: www.ltcpro4u.com
Specializing exclusively in LTC Planning since 1997, Phil is the top producer in Arizona and ranked 15th nationally.

Chapter 31

How To Use The Mindset Of The Prospect To Make The Sale

By Rob Cohen

$Q.$ *As part of my sales process, I want to remind prospects why they decided to look into purchasing LTCI. Do you have suggestions on how to use this approach when calling to set an appointment and how to weave it into my face-to-face presentation?*

Connecting prospects' current state of mind to what they were thinking when they initially inquired about LTCI is a very effective approach. Part of being a good salesperson is persuading people to act in their best interests based on their own thoughts and experiences.

Here Are Some Approaches To Use And Suggested Scripts -

Get people into the moment, and establish instant empathy. Assume they've had LTCI experiences. *"I understand. It's a tough issue to speak about. Everyone I speak to has a parent, grandparent, aunt, uncle, in-law or other relative who needed care outside the home or in-home by family or a health care specialist. So who was it in your family or was it your in-laws who had this experience?"*

Or if the prospect is single, say, *"Which of your parents, grandparents or other relatives needed some kind of care, even by the family, before they passed away?"*

When you get an answer, just ask a few questions about who needed care, what the ailment was and what kind of care was required. Then, empathize and validate by saying, *"I'm so sorry to hear that. Now I understand why you decided to address this. You're so smart to consider long term care issues while your health is, hopefully, at least stable."*

Begin health qualifying within a minute or two of starting the call. Do not ask permission to qualify health; it weakens you and your position. You may begin by saying, *"Nearly one-third of people with whom I speak wait too long to address LTCI. Unfortunately, they do not qualify for health reasons. Therefore, I need to ask you a few health questions to make sure I do not waste your time."*

Ask about any consequences of health issues. It's appropriate and necessary to make clients feel at least a little uncomfortable and vulnerable, so they will see the need to address the issue. *"How has your health been? What do you see as a possible consequence of your _____ (high blood pressure, diabetes, arthritis, osteoporosis, etc.) down the road?"*

There are two reasons to health qualify: 1) See if the prospects are eligible and should be pursued, and 2) Learn prospects' concerns and vulnerabilities. It doesn't matter if it was two weeks or six years ago; your job is to review their thought processes.

Ask questions beyond the normal health-qualifying queries. Do this after finding out about any health issue, even blood pressure, cholesterol, osteopenia, etc. and regardless of whether or not the prospects seem concerned about the issue.

Ask, *"Does this disease run in your family?"* If the answer is yes, say, *"No wonder you're addressing this, after learning that it runs in your family and before you have any complications."* If the answer is no, say, *"Wow, you are fortunate that it has not occurred in your family. However, we both know that health can change unexpectedly. It's good that you are considering LTCI now."*

Here are other questions that you can ask: What went through your mind when you were diagnosed with _____ condition? Were you surprised when the doctor told you that you had _____? If your friends or family told you the day before you found out that you were going to be diagnosed with xxx, what would you have told them?

At The Appointment

How can you establish prospect's need at the appointment and get them to move forward? Ask each spouse separately, *"Do you believe that you could need long term care insurance at some point in your life?"* If the answer is no or reflects ambivalence, review prospects' past experiences. You can use their relatives' need for LTCI and lack of planning as denial. Then, ask the question again. If the prospects' answer is yes, emphasize the importance of this acknowledgement. *"No wonder you didn't address this issue before today. Based on your past experiences, did self-insurance work? Is it important to you not to repeat what your family members went through and to avoid burdening your family with arranging and monitoring your care?"*

Another approach is, *"Given your health changes, did you believe that your health can change involuntarily, and at any time?"* Ask each spouse separately. *"How did you come to that conclusion?"*

Rob Cohen, CPA
Executive Vice-President – Sales: ACSIA Long Term Care/United Insurance Group (UIG).
Phone: 800-362-8837 x7070
Email: RCohen@ltcglobal.com
Website: www.ACSIA.com
Website: www.uiginc.com
After Rob's division achieved several years of dramatic LTC sales growth, Rob has returned to LTC Global to oversee all sales and operations for its ACSIA and UIG divisions.

Chapter 32

A Pre-Approach Letter That Works

By Trish Swanson

Q. *I'm planning to use direct mail leads and need a proven pre-approach letter for following up these new leads. What copy do you suggest I use?*

Using direct mail and following up leads first with a letter and then six days later with a phone call has worked extremely well for me. With the letter, I send a very poignant true story which relates how my mother needed help at home as a result of a leg amputation and several mild strokes.

I use such powerful and emotional copy as: *"I treasured my mother. I just didn't have the skills needed to care for her. The three of us siblings working together along with our two spouses weren't enough."* I conclude with, *"Don't confuse getting LTC insurance with someone not loving you enough. LTC insurance helps your kids get the care that will help them take better care of you. It allows the loved one the dignity that they have always asked for."*

Here are the letter and story I send to my direct mail leads.

My pre-approach letter

Thank you for your request for information on long term care planning. You probably did so because you are aware of the physical, emotional and financial devastation long term extended care can have on those you care about. People need extended care services because of accidents, health issues and age related issues. Planning before your health changes is essential since one out of every three people I talk to do not qualify for coverage. Plus, the cost of care is very high, and you are responsible for paying for these costs unless you plan ahead.

Please be expecting my phone call in the next few days. My responsibility is to help you determine if you need this type of protection and health qualify for coverage. Then I can help you shop for the best coverage at the best value and leave you with information so you have something to think about. **Plus, if you use the internet, we can review this without the need of meeting in person.**

I am a specialist in long term care, certified with the federal/state partnership programs and represent all the top insurance companies. Long-term care insurance is a **very affordable** way to address the risk of extended care. Since health insurance and Medicare (health insurance for those

65+) don't cover custodial care (which a majority of long term care is - help with activities of daily living), the cost and the burden is placed on you and your family.

My clients refer to long term care insurance as "nursing home avoidance protection" because it provides the resources to help you *receive care in your own home and avoid a nursing facility.*

Please find enclosed my personal story, an article and a brochure titled "Where Do I Start" for your review. You can also look at my bio online at www.trishswansonlongtermcare.com/contact. The American Association for Long Term Care Insurance lists me as one of the top Long Term Care Specialists in the nation. This experience and expertise helps make sure you get the appropriate information and recommendations without pressure or cost.

I am looking forward to speaking with you in the near future. Please be sure to ask me about any federal or state tax benefits that may be available in your situation.

Sincerely,
(I include my cell phone number, email address and website.)

Here is the copy that I use to share my personal story.

My story

"I treasured my mother...I just didn't have the skills needed to care for her."

I have always appreciated my parents since I was a child. I was always trying to give back to them because of how grateful I felt that they loved me so much and did such a good job raising me. When I was 16 I took a job for $1.25 an hour at a hotdog stand (much less than minimum wage at the time). I saved up my money for months and sent my parents on a plane trip to Florida to stay at the Polynesian Hotel in Disney World for their anniversary for three days and then to Daytona Beach for four days. I paid for that trip myself including sending flowers to their hotel room on their anniversary day. There's nothing I wouldn't do for my parents. I loved them so much.

When I was 19 and working downtown I won a first class ticket to Hawaii. I gave it to my parents for their anniversary present. My dad didn't want to go there so I went with my mom and paid my own fare to sit in coach class. We stayed for almost three weeks and had such a great time together. I loved my mom so much.

Later I married and visited them every week. It seemed my husband loved them as much as I did. Not too many years later, dad passed away from a massive heart attack. My mom was such a wonderful person I couldn't imagine not having her with us on our vacations. She was so much fun to be with. We didn't have her join us to babysit the kids. We never went out in the evenings unless she was with us. This was my mom. We both loved her so much.

I'm the baby of the family. I came along 11 years after my sister and 12 years after my brother. My sister was single and lived with my mom. My brother lived nearby as well and was married with three sons. I was married and had two sons as well. I would always tell my mom that she could move in with us if she ever needed to. I would always take care of her. I would certainly cook, clean, grocery shop and feed her. This was someone that I loved so much.

What I didn't understand was what she had tried to tell me for so many years. She never could get me to open my eyes. I was young and didn't have the knowledge to understand what was actually involved. She grew up as a child with a grandma who had suffered a stroke and lived in their living room for many years. It changed her whole childhood even though she wasn't the caregiver. My grandparents had all passed away before I was born. I never got to hear what it was like from their perspective. It's bad enough having anyone bathe you or wipe you. Now that I'm older I can see why my mom didn't want me to touch her private parts. I don't ever want my kids to touch me in that way. I'd rather have a caregiver do that and just have my kids there to visit me and cheer me. That's the way I want them to remember me. Love is a relationship between two people, not doing medical skills you're not trained for. Medical personnel only work eight hour shifts and go home to their families. They don't care for someone 24 hours a day, seven days a week and try to be there for their own family and perhaps a spouse as well. You can't be everything to everyone at once. I thought to myself, I am an adult; surely I could help my mom out if she needed it. This woman took such good care of me as a child. I loved her so much.

I was only 36 years old at the time she needed help. She had diabetes and had to have her leg amputated and had suffered a few mild strokes. There was nothing more that the hospital and doctors could do. She went back to her home with my sister. She wasn't capable of lifting herself or her hips. I sat next to her on the floor crying because I couldn't do the very thing I told her I would do. The words kept ringing in my ears (I'll take care of you…I love you) as I was covered in sweat from trying so hard to just move her. I didn't have the physical strength to lift her to move the diaper from under her body weight to change her. It took me over an hour. This is not like changing the diaper of an infant who's seven pounds. She was probably 120 pounds. I never had to try to lift dead weight before. Even a small child who's ready to begin walking lifts their hips for you when you're changing their diaper. I couldn't even move her from side to side to pull it out. Don't even talk about the mess I created attempting this and the discomfort I caused as I kept pulling on her body to accomplish this task. My own motherhood never prepared me for a situation like this. Unfortunately, my everything was not what she needed. She didn't just need someone to cook, clean, grocery shop and be a companion. I didn't have the necessary skills that my mom needed. There was nothing I wouldn't do for my mom. Unfortunately, there were things I couldn't do for my mom. It had nothing to do with love! I treasured my mother. I just didn't have the skills to care for her.

Did I mention the resentment that started wearing on me and my siblings after a few months? It seemed we were all questioning whether the other one was doing their fair share. Thank God it didn't escalate, but it was there. Heck, my own sister, who lived with my mom wasn't able to care for her even though she wasn't married and had no children. I only had to contend with this one day a week! I visited much more often but only had to do the physical care on Sunday. We had to hire a live-in caregiver (besides my sister who lived there), pay for home nursing visits, along with a ton of other things, all out of my mom's savings. We weren't trained medical professionals. We still needed help. Gee, that certainly didn't work out the way I had planned. I'm the one who kept telling her all along when she was healthy, "Don't worry mom…I'll take care of you."

I had a full time job that we depended on to pay the bills. My boss expected me to actually work and have my mind on my job when I was there. I had two children that needed my attention. My husband needed my attention as well. I was physically and emotionally exhausted. I couldn't be everything to everyone 24 hours a day. If I wasn't with my mom, I felt guilty. It affected my health. If only I had listened to her and worked with her to get long term care insurance while she was healthy. As usual, my mother was older and wiser than me.

Twelve years later I still feel guilty that I let her down those last six months. Did we cause her undo suffering from our inadequacies in moving her? I believe we did. I loved my mom so very deeply; I couldn't imagine not doing everything for her.

I still remember my 47-year-old brother wringing his hands, shaking his head, saying, *"Oh boy, what are we going to do?"* He said that out of sheer exasperation when he and my husband struggled together trying to lift mom out of bed, into the wheelchair and into the car to drive her to the doctor's office on the few occasions where a home health care nurse wasn't enough. The three of us siblings working together along with our two spouses wasn't enough.

Could my siblings and I change the decisions we made? No. But it did open my eyes and now I can share my story so that others aren't as blind as I was because after all…your children love you just as I loved my mom. Don't confuse getting long term care insurance with someone not loving you enough. Long term care insurance helps your kids get the type of care that will help them take better care of you. It provides for the needs that are necessary, which allows the kids time for loving, caring, touching and sharing memories. It allows the loved one the dignity that they have always asked for.

Feel free to give me a call at home at _____ if you'd like to discuss the impact this had on our family's lives.

Trish Swanson

LTCI Specialist, ACSIA Long Term Care
Phone: 800-515-4570
Email: trishswanson2001@aol.com
Website: www.trishswansonlongtermcare.com
Trish has been in the long term care insurance industry since 2000. She is considered one of the top LTCI specialists in the nation.

Chapter 33

Using The Five-Minute Sale To Generate Interest

By Susan Blais

Q. *Convincing prospects of the need for LTC insurance can be a long and challenging process. Have you found an easier and shorter way to accomplish this?*

By using what I have labeled "The Five Minute LTCI Sale" or "Selling LTCI Without A Struggle," in five minutes I can discuss the critical issues of LTCI with prospects and determine if they are interested in pursuing the subject further. It allows me to present the true value of LTCI simply and quickly.

Here are the key points I discuss:

Point 1 - It is very likely that you will live a long life. It shouldn't be too difficult for your prospects to admit that they are likely to live a long life. Because of that,

Point 2 - It is very likely that you will need LTC. In 2010, every person who reaches age 65 has *at least* a fifty percent chance of needing long-term care. And the longer we live, the greater the likelihood. Who wants to bet their future on the toss of a coin?

Point 3 - It will be very expensive and the cost today is not your problem. It's for the inflated cost sometime in the future – 20 or 30 years from now that you must plan ahead to provide those needed dollars.

Point 4 – You have limited choices as to how to pay these costs.

- You will pay personally out of your hard-earned retirement money,

- You will become a ward of the state

- Or you can transfer the risk to an insurance company. You take the risk or let the insurance company do it!

Point 5 - The real value of this policy is not the dollars it will provide today, but the dollars to pay your claim when you need it – down the road. How much money is going to be there when you need it?

Close – Is this a topic that you think we should discuss further?

The Five Minute Sale includes a formula that helps prospects see that transferring the risk to an insurance company is the most cost-effective way to go. It shows how much LTC will cost when they need it; and, most importantly, it shows the premium in relation to the pool of money that will be available when the client needs care.

The formula is simple. Begin with the cost of care in your region today. Then factor in your prospect's age today and a projection of when they are likely to need care. Based on industry claims data, most people do not need LTC until their mid-80's.

Then apply a rate of inflation to your calculations. While we know that the historical inflation rate in this sector is close to six percent compounded, we use five percent because that is what we have to sell in today's policies. It also allows us to say to the prospect that our calculations are on the conservative side.

Finally, according to the recent claims studies, the vast majority of claims fall into the three to five year range. Using this information, you can provide a context for prospects to make an informed decision.

Here's how it's calculated: The Benefit Pool (when you go on claim) x The Daily Benefit Sold Today x The Number of Years (Days) Sold x The Inflation Option Chosen x Length of Time Until the Claim = Economic Benefit of the Policy (Face Amount).

Here's a specific example. A client age 57 purchases a LTCI policy. The current cost of care is $200 per day. The client purchases a five year benefit (1825 days) with five percent compounded inflation protection. The initial benefit pool is $365,000.

Next, what is the benefit pool when they will need the care? Start with the initial benefit pool of $365,000, projected first claim at age 85, typical claim of three to five years and rate of inflation benefit of five percent. Thus, if the client goes on claim at age 85, the benefit pool is worth $1,430,000!

To take the formula a step further, rather than saying, *"Mr. Johnson, the premium is only $3500 and for that you're getting $200 a day,"* you can now put the premium rate into a context that will be more appealing to the prospect: *"For $3500 a year, you will be receiving over a million dollars of coverage."*

Marketing Tip: You can let your clients and prospects know you have a way to calculate their individual risk for LTC in an email, letter and flyer on your website. This gets their attention and allows you to open the LTC conversation. The Five Minute Sale technique quickly separates the "planners" from the "deniers", saving you time and boosting your closing ratio.

Susan Blais, LTCP
Barry J. Fisher Insurance Marketing Inc.
Phone: 818-444-7757
Email: susanb@paradigmins.com
Website: www.bjfim.com
Susan manages the LTCI sales team and creates sales and marketing materials to help independent agents promote LTCI to their clients.

Chapter 34

Avoiding Sticker Shock And Creating Value

By Matt McCann

Q. *My prospects are frequently shocked at the cost of the policy. How can I effectively respond to that?*

Many times agents create sticker shock for their prospects, which can cause the prospect to respond, "I have to think about it." Even though the agent has created need and urgency, when prospects are shown the policy recommendations, they may start to focus on the cost of the premium, not the cost of current and future care.

Sometimes this happens when an agent doesn't ask the proper financial questions. Some agents say they feel uncomfortable asking such questions. However, it's their fiduciary responsibility to do this. How can an agent make recommendations about an asset protection product without knowing the amount of assets the prospect is protecting? In addition, we have to understand affordability.

It comes down to the physiological impact a perceived high premium has on the client. Show two proposals that are based on what you hear at the appointment. The first one is a very affordable plan. The second one is the plan you think is the best option for the client. For analytical clients, perhaps show a third plan, which would be the luxury plan.

You show the basic plan first. It's very affordable, won't scare the client and will keep them paying attention. However, you must create value. Do that by saying, *"Mr. and Mrs. Smith, I have two great options for you. First, based on your health and age, I am recommending Mutual of Vegas. Now, I represent all the top insurance companies, so if you have a favorite let me know, but Mutual of Vegas represents, in your situation, the best coverage at the best value."*

"The first plan is a basic plan. It provides for $3000 a month of benefits, a two year pool of money and inflation." Be sure to explain the "pool," CPI, 3% compound, etc. *"Now, $3000 a month will not cover all your long term care needs. However, based on the current cost of home care in your area which is $17 an hour, $3000 a month, in today's dollars, would provide you with 176 hours of home care each month. Do you think 176 hours of home care that is paid by Mutual of Vegas would help you stay in your own home and relieve some of the burden on your family?"*

The client will say *"yes."* You continue, *"The second plan provides you with a lot more breathing room, which means it allows for more flexibility."* Then explain the monthly benefit, shared care, etc. *"What that means to you, Mr. and*

Mrs. Smith, is the extra money would provide you with 276 hours of home care being paid for by Mutual of Vegas each and every month. That is 100 more hours every month. That amount of home care would certainly make sure you can stay in your own home and allow your family to be loving and supportive, without creating a huge physical, emotional and financial burden on them. Don't you think that this is true?" Confirm this with clients. *"It would also make sure you can live in a quality assisted living facility and help you avoid a nursing home, a fact which you stated was important to you. And, if you do have to go to a nursing home, you have the resources to pay for a quality facility."*

Move to the close

Then move to your close. I always use the "Biggest Mistake" close. (See the next chapter, which explains this close.) I don't ask them which plan they want. The last thing I ask, after writing the application, is which plan do they want to apply for?

You will see that many clients will talk you into buying more than the basic plan. They will say, *"Matt, don't you think we really need more than xxxx a month in benefits?"* You respond, *"That's really a good point."* Many times they will move up from your basic plan to the plan you really wanted them to purchase or something in between.

When the client starts talking that way, you know they have bought into the whole idea of transferring the LTC risk with the insurance, thus making this a solid sale. You, as the agent, also don't come across as a car salesperson, having to keep lowering your original plan to meet their price point, assuming you were even given the chance to do that.

The point is we create value after developing need and urgency, without scaring the client with a high premium.

Sometimes you hear agents talk to clients saying things like, *"I know LTC insurance is expensive."* Why would anyone ever do that? Who says it's expensive? Expensive compared to what? I think an agent should always say, *"LTC insurance is very affordable and can be designed to fit your needs and budget. It's also much less expensive than paying for your future care yourself."*

Matt McCann
Director of Business Development at ACSIA Long Term Care
Phone: 630-698-0916
Email: mmccann@ltcglobal.com
Website: www.ltcopportunity.com
A former LTC insurance top producer, Matt has developed selling techniques and sales strategies that have been adopted by ACSIA nationally.

Chapter 35

The Biggest Mistake: A Close For Clients Considering Self Insuring

By Harry Crosby

Q. *I work with many prospects who can afford to self insure. Do you have a close to recommend that works in those situations?*

Many people think they can self insure. Closing these prospects and convincing them that this insurance makes good economic sense can be tough if you are not prepared. If they can self insure, why wouldn't they just take their chances? I have found that my method – which I call "The Biggest Mistakes" - works very well.

Here is what I say to prospects: There are really only two mistakes you can make with long term care.

Mistake Number One - You get one of these plans. It doesn't matter which one. You buy a plan, pay every year, live a long happy and healthy life, die in your sleep with a smile on your face and the money you paid in is…

You now pause, and many times they will answer by saying the money is gone. Right, the money you paid in is gone. Had you known that this would be the case, you would never get a policy.

Mistake Number Two - You stay self insured – which is what you are right now. Then one or both of you need care. Not only do you pay for it yourself out of your pocket, but the rest of the burden is placed on your family.

Let's look at the two mistakes.

Let's say you get this plan, and your premium is about $1800 a year. You live another 30 years, and at age 85 you die in your sleep with a smile on your face - never needing a day of care and thus never getting a dime out of the policy. You get to the pearly gates, they look at your file and they laugh at you, because you made a $54,000 mistake for having this policy and never needing it. By the way, that amount is considerably less than one year of care in today's dollars.

Now, mistake number two. You decide to not get this policy and roll the dice. Twenty years from now, when you are 75, you need care just for three years. You pay for the care out-of-pocket. Based on past trends, the average cost of care will be about $435,000 or much more if you live longer - which most people do.

It is now crystal clear which mistake is the biggest. Your family may not have noticed the relatively small premium you paid for this coverage, but they are acutely aware of the tremendous cost you are now paying for care. The question for you today is which mistake do you want to take a chance of making - spending an amount you would hardly notice or face the rising cost of long term care that could rise to more than a half a million dollars using the funds you work all your life to build. I hope I make the mistake of choosing long term care insurance and never having to use it. What about you, Mr. Prospect?

The response - That is why top financial advisors and the federal and state government encourage people like you to look into LTCI. It is just common sense.

Harry Crosby, LTCP
President, Crosby Solutions, Inc
Phone: 803-920-0930
Email: ltcauthor@yahoo.com
Website: www.long-termcareinsurance.com
Harry has over 20 years of experience in LTC Insurance Sales. He is the author of *Long Term Care Insurance - the complete guide* and an informational brochure entitled "Should I buy Long Term Care Insurance? Or do I prefer Crisis Management?"

Chapter 36

The Real Cost Of Waiting

By Harry Crosby

Q. I know that it definitely makes sense to purchase LTC insurance at a younger age instead of waiting. How can I effectively explain those advantages to prospects?

If clients ever expect to own a LTC insurance policy, it's much better to purchase it now while the premiums are affordable. It makes no sense to wait.

Delaying purchasing a long term care policy can ultimately prevent coverage, or render coverage to be cost prohibitive. The mistake many prospects make is when they compare today's premiums for a 50-year-old to today's premiums for a 65-year-old today. Then they decide to wait until they're 65 and save the money they would have spent on the premium.

Let's use the example of a 50-year-old versus that same 50 year old waiting until he or she is age 65. I'm using five percent compound inflation benefit in my calculations.

Age 50		Age 65	
Monthly Benefit Maximum Now	$5,000	Monthly Benefit Maximum in 15 years	$10,000
Annual Premium	$3,474.18	Annual Premium	$10,100.94

During the 15 years, from age 50 to age 65, the policy with a five percent inflation protection rider doubles in benefits. So in order to match the same policy that could have been purchased 15 years earlier, one would have to calculate the premium based on a $10,000 monthly benefit at age 65.

Then, let's assume that both live to age 90 and die suddenly without using the policy. The 50-year-old would have paid premiums for 35 years, and the 65-year-old would have paid premiums for only 20 years. The 50-year-old purchaser would have paid a total of $121,596.30 during his life time, but the 65-year-old purchaser who waited would have paid a total of $202,018.80 - an additional $80,422.50 and received 15 years less coverage.

The factors that could change and affect one's ability to purchase in 15 years are:

- Premiums rates on new policies are usually higher than the premiums on the policy that was replaced.

- Underwriting standards will probably get more restrictive. Even if one qualifies now for coverage, he or she may not qualify later because of the changes in underwriting.

- Cost of care continues to rise year after year.

- Rates are based on age and significantly increase as one gets older.

- Your health might change, rendering you ineligible for the coverage or ineligible for discounts.

- Spouses may become ineligible because of poor health. This would increase the premiums at the time of purchase because of ineligibility for a spouse discount.

Harry Crosby, LTCP

President, Crosby Solutions, Inc
Phone: 803-920-0930
Email: ltcauthor@yahoo.com
Website: www.long-termcareinsurance.com
Harry has over 20 years of experience in LTC insurance Sales. He is the author of *Long Term Care Insurance - the complete guide* and an informational brochure entitled "Should I buy Long Term Care Insurance? Or do I prefer Crisis Management?"

PART 5

Marketing Advice From LTC Experts

Chapter 37

The ABCs Of Selling Online

By Amy Pollock

Q. *I'm hearing that some agents are selling over the internet. How do they do it?*

I have been selling online, meaning over the phone and by webinar, since 2005. As baby boomers have aged and become our market, and I am one, we want it fast. Forget coming to my home. I found that "meeting" on the internet, where we have a live meeting with screen sharing, is an efficient, easy and very well received means to create new clients.

Screen sharing - I take prospects to my private online website where they can view my screen on their computers. If they have a speaker phone, they can watch hands-free and listen as we discuss LTCI. Connectivity is simple. It even works for people in their 70's who aren't as computer savvy. The feedback has been that it's easy, simple and appreciated.

Benefits to the consumer - Prospects are able to obtain information without having to schedule an appointment in their home. Arranging appointments is easy; and, at the end of the meeting, the agent emails all proposals and brochures to the client. For prospects, benefits include speed, ease, thoroughness and no perceived pressure. I now have more success in setting appointments, having online meetings and closing sales.

Here's what I do when calling a prospect.

Scheduling the appointment - Everything I ask or say has a purpose. One of my key talking points is that: *"There is a lot to know about long term care. This is not like any other kind of insurance where you choose plan A, B or C. Here you have quite a number of options. Understanding how to make the right choices for your needs is most important. One of the biggest mistakes buyers can make is to overbuy coverage and spend more money than necessary. My job is to help you not to do that."*

Let that hang in the air for an extra second; then, review their health and ask for the appointment. To remove the unknown of what you're going to do, always tell people what to expect. Explain, *"Here's how the process works. We will set an appointment for a private online meeting with you both. It will take about 45 minutes to one hour. Once you log on, we will use screen sharing. I'll show you how LTCI policies work, what options are available and how to trigger the benefits. Then we will do side-by-side comparisons of costs from all the top companies. We can even design a plan to fit a specific budget. When we are finished, you will be able to make a good decision for yourselves. Sound fair?"*

Then, it is a matter of scheduling a time to meet. Be sure that husband and wife are both on board.

Confirm the appointment - I always email a confirmation of the appointment, repeat the agenda for the meeting and include the link to the website with log on instructions. The closing line of the email is, "I look forward to working with you (both) and helping to plan for your long term care issues."

The appointment - Call at the appointed time. Be punctual. The clients will double click on the link, and then I provide the session key. Our computers attach, and we view jointly my PowerPoint presentation. The presentation must be focused, concise and cannot include an abundance of statistics. At the beginning, I present a picture of myself on the screen so the clients know to whom they're speaking.

Your voice - When meeting in person, we intuitively use body language and eye contact to make a point. However, in the world of online sales, you use your voice for emphasis. You must speak more slowly, lower the pitch of your voice and periodically pause. This creates the impact of the point you are making. Your voice is the orchestra. This is a new technique, but it can produce great results.

The sales presentation - I begin by reviewing the agenda for our call, and then start the PowerPoint. My job is to explain each slide, not to read it. Each bullet point appears one at a time, so clients cannot get ahead of me. I invite them to interrupt with questions. Make sure to check in frequently by asking, *"Any questions? Does this make sense? Was that clear?"* However, don't do it too often so as to be annoying, but with enough frequency to be sure the clients haven't dozed off.

As we discuss the cost of care, I always ask if it makes sense to *"put someone else's money under yours, to protect your own money"* and then wait for an answer from each person. I will not budge from that slide and move into the rate illustrations until I have a verbal agreement from both parties on the phone.

Plan design - Once I have that agreement, I then go to the illustration software and select options. When we've completed one illustration from one company, I ask if we are in "a ballpark that makes sense for them" and wait for an answer. Once you get their price point, you can make any adjustments to meet their budget and then show them other companies in side-by-side comparisons.

Closing - *"Okay, all you can decide to do today is apply. If you're comfortable and serious, then let's start the process. Today is (date). If you apply today, you probably won't be approved, if we're lucky, until late next month, perhaps later. It will take another ten days for your policy to be printed and sent to me. I will send it to you, and you will have 30 days to review it and make adjustments. If you change your mind, you will get a full and prompt refund. So, that puts us out close to three months. Can you decide by then? Does that give you enough time?"*

This is not a hard close, because if I did my job right, I've closed all along the way. The clients know what they want to do before I even say it. My placement rate has been very acceptable, and I am careful not to use this approach as a crutch to close the sale.

Closing for a first call - If the clients are ready to apply, simply say, *"Okay, here's what I'm going to need: a list of your medication, dosages, your doctor's name, address and phone number, and one of your children's contact information as a third party back-up. I will call you back in five minutes to complete the application on the phone. I will fedex everything to you with sign and date stickers and enclose a prepaid return fedex envelope for you to send it back promptly."*

Closing for a second call - About half of my sales are first call closes, but some will need a little more time. For them, I suggest saying, *"How about if I call you in three days? All I ask is that you start discussing this when we hang up while the information is fresh. Then when I call you back, you will know what you want to do."* I get a commitment from the clients, and we agree on a call-back time. The subliminal message is that I expect a decision when I call them back.

The follow-up - Two weeks after I submit the applications, my assistant emails my new clients on a weekly basis to give a status report of what's happening with their application(s). If we need help from them getting doctor's records, we'll ask for it. It's very good to keep in touch as the process moves along. Let clients know what's going on, and be available to address questions or concerns right away. When clients are approved, inform them immediately.

Today, over 90 percent of my business is sold in this manner, and my market is no longer limited to my local area. When I was conducting appointments in person, I averaged nearly 25,000 business miles annually and sold in one state. Now, I drive 4,000 miles annually and sell in many states. The price of gas and time wasted driving support online sales as a desirable selling avenue. If you will become as effective in selling online as in face-to-face meetings, you can grow your business significantly.

Amy Pollock

Founding Partner, Specialist LTC, LTC Financial Partners, LLC
Phone: 404-237-1189
Email: amy.pollock@ltcfp.net
Website: amypollock.ltcfp.com
Amy has spent over 16 years in LTCI sales. She has written for national newspapers and magazines on the issue of effective planning and believes that, today, our consumer lifestyles and longer healthier lives combine to make advance planning essential.

Chapter 38

How Our Male and Female Brains Affect How We Buy Long Term Care Insurance

By Holly Buchanan

Q. *Do differences in female and male brains affect how individuals buy LTCI? If yes, how?*

A couple comes into your office. As you discuss LTCI options, you notice a difference in the types of information they want from you.

The husband wants to know:
- How much a policy would cost and what kind of coverage he can expect?

- What would happen if he never uses the policy?

The wife wants to know:
- How much a policy would cost and what coverage it would provide?

- Exactly what kind of care is covered?

- If the policy includes a care coordinator, who will be there as a resource to help her make good decisions?

- The history of the insurance company and what guarantees she has that the company will still be around when she or her husband needs care?

- Where she can go to look at reviews of the company?

- What kind of policy choices she has and what the differences are between the policies?

Welcome to the difference between male and female decision making styles! Her female brain wants more information, wants to plan ahead to avoid problems and wants guarantees of safety and security. She has a more deliberate decision making process. Her husband's decision process is based on numbers, goals and opportunities. He is using his male brain to focus on an end goal and a linear way to achieve that goal.

Many sales are lost because of misunderstandings about how men and women make buying decisions. We all notice the differences between men and women in our personal lives. Many of those same differences are at work in the workplace and in sales situations.

There's a wealth of new research on brain differences between men and women. These differences have a direct impact on how we make financial decisions, including buying LTCI. So let's use the facts to create a more effective sales presentation for both women and men.

Before I jump in, let me make one thing clear. There are proven differences between men and women. There is no suggestion that one is better than the other. Also, not all men think alike and not all women think alike. Some women may have more of a male decision making style, while some men may relate more to a female decision making style. But there are some general differences that are important to understand and which can make a huge difference in how effective you are as a sales person.

Overview of brain differences

There is amazing new research on brain differences between men and women. Scientists put men and women in an MRI and watched different parts of their brains light up when subjects processed information and made decisions.

In his book *Leadership and The Sexes, Using Gender Science to Create Success In Business,* Michael Gurian points out that neurobiologists have been able to track over 100 biological differences between the male and female brain[1]. These differences are important because how we use our brains affects how we experience the world, how we make decisions, what we buy and why we buy it, including financial services. In a selling situation, men and women may require different information, presented in a slightly different manner based on how their brains operate.

Here are some of the main brain differences and how those differences affect our perception and decision making process whether choosing a financial advisor or buying a financial product. Again, these generalities won't apply to everyone, but it's helpful to understand the distinctions.

Men's Decision Making Process	Women's Decision Making Process
1. Process quickly	1. Process completely
• Want to take action	• Want to think it through
• Use compartmentalized thinking	• Use holistic thinking
• Prioritize options	• Compare options
• Focus on immediate gains	• Focus on long-term benefits
• Use short-term planning	• Use long-term planning
• Focus on achieving goals	• Focus on achieving goals and avoiding bad outcomes
• Motivated by rewards	• Motivated by consequences

Conclusion #1: Men process quickly. Women process completely.

One of my favorite stories about the differences between men and women is the story of the Rabbi and his wife. The Rabbi describes the way his wife tackles obstacles as full of drama. She rages. She cries. She internalizes everything. Her system of problem-solving takes a long time and involves making everything personal and leading with her emotions in a quest to see how she would feel about each possible solution. It is apparently a very stressful process. In contrast, the Rabbi's problem-solving method is to just try to find the fastest fix. Yet, he prefers his wife's method. When asked why, he said it was because, "Her decisions always end up being the right ones, whereas mine always end up being the quick ones."[2]

A common frustration I hear from sales people is that women can't make a decision. It's not that women can't make a decision; it's simply that women often have a more deliberate decision making process. Women tend to want more information before they make a decision. Many sales people I interview remark that women ask more questions in the sales process. Why is this?

Brain difference A - Men are hard wired to take action. Women are hard wired to think through a problem.

Researchers have found differences in how men and women use their brains to react to different situations, especially in response to stress and anger. When men are stressed and face challenges, they want to take action. When women are stressed, they want to gather the wagons and talk it through.

Men's externally focused brains, in conjunction with testosterone, often trigger an action response. Think "fight or flight." In women, their internal focused brains, in combination with estrogen and oxytocin, a bonding hormone, trigger a "tend and befriend" response.

Brain difference B - Men use compartmentalized thinking. Women use holistic thinking.

Women have more connections between the right and left hemispheres of the brain.   They are often pulling on both sides of their brains when making decisions. In contrast, men tend to have more compartmentalized brains, often using one side of the brain or the other. They focus on one thing at a time and don't like to be distracted. With their efficient, focused brains, men want to narrow down their options until they find one solution that solves the immediate problem.

Women tend to multi-task, moving easily from one task to another, often juggling several plates in the air at once. With their more holistic brains, women often pull in more criteria, expanding the search to find the solution that meets as many needs as possible. Women also tend to have longer checklists of things that matter to them when making a buying decision, like buying LTCI. That longer checklist of what matters leads to more questions and more research during the buying process.

Example: Choosing a financial advisor
Men:

- What are his/her credentials?

- What kind of a track record does he/she have?

- What's his/her investment strategy?

- What are his/her fees?

Women:

- What are his/her credentials?

- What kind of a track record does he/she have?

- What's his/her investment strategy?

- What are his/her fees?

- Does he/she work with people like me?

- What experience have others had working with this person?

- How much money do we need to invest with him/her in order to get truly personal attention?

- How much communication can I expect?

- What are his/her values?

- Can I trust this person?

- What if this person leaves his/her current company?

- What if this company goes bankrupt?

- Is this someone I feel safe with, or will he/she be judgmental about our current situation?

- Will he/she use a lot of technical jargon, or will he/she speak to me like a human being?

Women want many of the same things as men, they just want more. By meeting her longer checklist, you're also satisfying him as well. The extra information she gathers can help both of them feel more confident in the decision.

Brain difference C - Men prioritize. Women compare.

Men have more gray matter, women have more white matter. In human brains, gray matter represents information processing centers, whereas white matter works to network these processing centers. He's designed to process quickly. She's designed to process completely. (Remember the story of the Rabbi and his wife?) He's prioritizing; she's comparing all the options. Expect that closing the sale with the woman may take more time as she sorts through all the ways this purchase will affect her life and family.

When selling LTCI, understand that women may want more information than men. She may ask more questions and have more concerns. She may need to process information and then set up another meeting to make a final decision.

For men:
- Always have an agenda for the meeting and clearly state the action you want to take by the end of the meeting.

- Give him an executive summary and bullet point the most important information.

- Tie LTCI to a goal he has clearly stated. For example, if he has a specific goal of wanting control over what kind of care he receives and where he receives it, LTCI can provide him that control while other options, like Medicaid, won't.

- If one of his goals is to be smart with his money, share a scenario where one man has LTCI and another does not and show the financial consequences. Paint a vivid picture of the "smart man" and how he used the insurance company's money, versus the second man who had to spend a large amount of his own money.

For women:

- Share stories of how this has affected other people like her who are in similar situations.

- Discuss her family situation and responsibilities.

- Be prepared for lots of questions. Share more information if she wants it, and take extra time to answer all her questions and concerns.

- Talk specifics. She may want to know more about what kind of care the policy specifically covers.

- Give her time to process information, and then come back at a separate meeting for the couple to make a final decision. While he may want to narrow down options and take an immediate action, she may want to compare all her options and think it through.

Conclusion #2 - Men want an immediate gain. Women want long term benefits.

My friend Michele was buying a big screen TV with her husband. He wanted to buy it so that weekend they could watch the game on the new TV. She wanted to buy it for Thanksgiving, many months in the future. When the family came over, everyone could watch the game on the big screen TV together.

Brain difference D - Men focus on short-term planning. Women focus on long-term planning.

There's an area at the front of the brain involved in long term planning, including problem solving, emotion, judgment and complex thought. It also measures future consequences of current actions. In *Brain Rules*, John Medina points to research that this area is slightly thicker in women[3].

Researchers are still debating what this means. We know from evolution that men, the hunters, needed to focus on immediate needs, while women, the gatherers and caretakers, needed to plan ahead to make sure they had enough food for the winter and had everything they needed to care for children and family. Some of this ancient hard-wiring may still be at work.

Selling LTCI

Women are doing a lot of long term planning and comparing many options to find the best option to meet their needs now and in the future. Women may value the future benefits of LTCI more than men do.

For men:

- If there is an immediate benefit, let him know. For example, if he is healthy enough now to get a good rate, that may not be true in another few years and he'll pay a lot more.

For women:

- Include the woman in any long term planning or insurance discussions. She may be your biggest ally. Insurance can be a tough sell because most people think they won't see benefits for years or even decades, if they see benefits at all. Men, especially, struggle with this. Women, with their long term planning and focus on being prepared are a perfect fit for insurance products. They may be better able to see and focus on the long term benefit.

- Be sure to address her fear that the insurance company may no longer be around or able to pay the claim 20 or 30 years down the road.

Conclusion #3 - Men are focused on achieving goals. Women are focused on achieving goals and avoiding bad outcomes.

Men focus on *"how do I get there?"* Woman focus on *"how do I get there? And, what could go wrong along the way?"* Women tend to focus more on risks. Note that I am not saying women are necessarily risk averse. They're more risk aware, focusing on safety and security.

In my 2010 Women and Finance Survey, I gave women a choice of which article they wanted to read - "The Four

Secrets to Having the Retirement of your Dreams," or "The Four Biggest Mistakes in Retirement Planning and How to Avoid Them." Here are the results:

Women under 50:
- The four biggest mistakes and how to avoid them – 55%
- The four secrets to the retirement of your dreams – 30%
- Neither – 15%

Women over 50:
- The four biggest mistakes and how to avoid them – 42%
- The four secrets to the retirement of your dreams – 30%
- Neither – 28%

In both surveys, the majority of women chose "The Four Biggest Mistakes and How to Avoid Them." When it comes to financial planning, women don't want to make a mistake. They look at what might go wrong, and want to make sure they are protected. A lot of financial advertising is about achieving goals. I'm not saying that's a bad thing, but there are opportunities to create marketing materials that also address preventing bad outcomes.

Brain difference D - Men have an active reward center. Women have an active consequence center.

In a research study, men and women played an investment game while their brains were scanned by an MRI. In men, the reward center of the brain lit up as did the area that calculates numbers. In women, the reward center lit up, but so did the worry and error detection center. Women continued to think about the game and the consequences.[4] This is important. Men focused on the rewards. Women focused on the rewards but also the consequences.

Research in this area is ongoing, but studies show gender differences in the worry, anxiety and error detection areas of the brain. This could directly affect why women are more risk aware and less willing to take risks than men.

Selling to men

When you're selling LTCI to men, you're often met with resistance. In his mind, he is probably thinking, *"That's not going to happen to me."* He is focused on achieving his financial goals and doesn't want to spend money on something he's probably never going to use.

If he does accept that something might happen, his response is usually, *"If something happens to me, my wife/daughters/family can take care of me."* Or, *"I'll pay for it myself."* Again, he may not have really thought through what an event would look like, what kind of care he would need, or how much it would really cost.

Women also suffer from the *"It won't happen to me"* syndrome. But with their brain hard-wired to plan ahead and avoid bad outcomes, they may be more likely to sit down and really think through what an event would look like, who would provide the care, probably her, and how much it could actually cost.

For men:

- Share a story of a husband who got LTCI and one who didn't and look at the different outcomes. Educate him on costs and what an actual event looks like. He probably has not painted that picture in his mind. Paint it for him.

For women:

- Stress how LTCI can protect her retirement plan. She has probably thought through what an incident would look like, how much it would cost and how quickly it could deplete their retirement portfolio.

- Talk about the effects on families of becoming primary care givers. Women don't want to burden loved ones with their care. Talk about the consequences to caregivers.

- Ask women, *"What are your concerns?"* and then sit back and listen.

More brain research is being conducted every day, and we continue to be amazed by what we're learning. The differences between men's and women's brains affect everything we do, including how we make financial decisions.

Again, let me stress that these are generalities. But understanding how our brains are wired and how that affects our decision making process can be an incredibly valuable tool when selling LTCI. Understand how men and women think, and you will close more sales.

Holly Buchanan

Buchanan Marketing, LLC
Email: holly@hollybuchanan.com
Website: www.sellingfinancialservicestowomen.com
Holly is a specialist in marketing and selling financial services to women and couples. She is the author of *Selling Financial Services to Women - What Men Need to Know and Even Women Will Be Surprised to Learn* and co-author of *The Soccer Mom Myth - Today's Female Consumer: Who She Really Is, Why She Really Buys.*

FOOTNOTES

[1] *Pg. xx, Leadership and The Sexes Michael Gurian with Barbar Annis, 2008*
[2] *Http://lifestyle.msn.com/relationships/article.aspx?cpdocumentid=2 4375124&Gtl=32023*
[3] *Brain Rules by John Medina, pg. 247*
[4] *Research study by Colin Camerer, at Cal-Tech, and Read Montague, at Baylor College of Medicine.- http://scienceblogs.com/cortex/2009/ 03/men_vs_women.php*

Chapter 39

Tips On How To Successfully Sell LTCI To Women

By Deborah Peterson

Q. *How can I improve my technique when selling to women?*

Long term care insurance is a perfect fit for women. Think about it. Throughout time, a woman's role has been that of caregiver, first taking care of her husband and children and then her parents and in-laws.

According to a study by a major carrier, one of the top four financial concerns for women is protecting themselves against unforeseen circumstances, like a LTC event. That same study showed that over 21 percent of women surveyed plan to buy LTC insurance in the next three years.

So what kills sales with women? According to Connie Podesta, in her new book, *Make a Fortune Selling to Women*, many skilled, intelligent salespeople don't realize that some of the most elusive deal breakers may be originating from the gender lens which they and their customer look through. Ms. Podesta explains that a woman wants her shopping experience to be a personal, productive, professional, positive experience that makes her feel part of the process.

Women like to talk. Look at this as a positive part of the process. Ask the client open-ended questions about herself and her family. What, when, where, why and how? Here are some examples: Do you have children? How many? Where do they live? What kind of work do they do? Grandchildren? If you require some kind of care, what role do you think your children will play?

You are doing a few things here. First, you are getting your client to think about LTC from a personal perspective. Second, you are learning about her support system. Women who have children don't want to be a burden to them.

Those who don't have children are concerned about who is going to provide their care; your approach to selling to these women may need to be a little different.

Women are concerned about outliving their money. Ask your client about her money. How much do you have? Where is it? What kind of an investor are you? How do you feel about your money? What is your money for? How important is leaving an estate to your children? What are your sources of income? How will that change?

You must find out what's important to your client. What keeps her awake at night? Where does she find enjoyment?

The deeper you probe, the more successful your efforts will be. Focus on becoming an advocate in securing this coverage for the client, rather than on closing the sale. Women need time to make decisions. Nurture your relationship. For women, it's all about connecting with you, your business and others.

Deborah Peterson
Peterson LTC, Inc.
Phone: 425-788-6239
Email: Deborah@petersonltc.com
Website: www.petersonltc.com
Deborah is a leading LTC solutions specialist for nearly 15 years. She is affiliated with ACSIA Long Term Care.

Chapter 40

Personal Letters From Those On Claim

By Mark Goldberg & Matt McCann

Q. *As part of my sales presentation, I want to include a personal story about a claim that an LTC carrier is paying and the benefits for the client and the family. Do you have a letter that I can show prospects?*

Sharing how the benefits really do work when a client goes on claim and how grateful people are is a powerful way to help convey the need. We shared the contents of several letters at a recent agent conference. These letters are a compilation of a number of letters received by several carriers.

Here are excerpts from these letters. We did change the names of the letter writer and the state to protect their privacy.

Letter 1 – Her husband has Alzheimer's

I want to thank all of you and everyone at the insurance company too and recognize the professionalism of the claims staff for all of their assistance in helping me deal with my husband's battle with Alzheimer's disease. We've been married for over 40 years, and I never dreamed we would have to go through this. Tom was first diagnosed with short term memory loss, and then we learned it was Alzheimer's. I remember feeling so scared and vulnerable.

The claims staff at the insurance company really helped me understand what kind of options Tom and I might have here where we live in Utah. There were services I simply didn't know were available. For that matter, even our doctor didn't know they were available. As my husband's memory faded faster, it became very apparent I couldn't keep him at home. Tom got angry and frustrated, and his actions became so unpredictable. He could no longer drive, and our lives changed so very much.

I also have the responsibility of taking care of my frail 95-year-old mother in addition to my husband. This policy has allowed me to not only get the help I need, but also to get a break from time to time. Because of having this policy, it's nowhere near the nightmare it could have been if I had to face this all alone.

When we got this policy my husband was afraid it was just going to be a waste of money - that we would never use it. I have learned no one can know what will happen. As a result of what has happened to us, I've seen others who have had to go through this and not have a policy. They have a lot less options than we do, and it causes families to fight and all kinds of other stress.

Thank god for this policy and for having such a program like this. I can only hope everyone does something to protect themselves when they can. I recommend it to everyone I know. Thank you so very much.

Letter 2 – From a claimant's husband

We bought our policy when we were 60. My wife Emily had a stroke when she was 64. The stroke left her partially paralyzed, and we were devastated. She required care to just cope with the stuff you have to do every day to live. If it wasn't for this insurance, she would have gone into a nursing home permanently. But because she had this protection, we could bring help into the house. We didn't have to change the way we lived. Without the policy, I would have been the one who provided the care and my daughter would have had to quit her job to help me.

Because we had this policy, it prevented us from having to change our lives; and that made all the difference in the world. As far as I am concerned the value of having the policy is priceless. It's probably the best investment we have ever made.

Letter 3 – Written by claimant's daughter and son

We didn't even know that mom and dad had long term care insurance until they both got sick. This policy made helping them find the best care for their circumstances so much easier.

We had no idea how flexible their policies were. The fact they had the choice of going into Hyatt assisted living facility instead of a nursing home has given us both great relief. We might not have that option if we didn't know we would have the dollars the policy provides them for the care.

My brother and I have both applied for coverage for ourselves as we have experienced firsthand what the impact of having these policies can have. My parents never wanted to be a burden, and I don't want to be a burden to my kids.

I am a mother of two teenage children; and if I had to be the one who had to coordinate and provide my parents' care, it would make my life impossible. My brother is in a similar situation.

Mark Goldberg

LTC Solutions Specialist

Email: mgoldb3181@aol.com

Starting as a producer in 1991 Mark has become a prominent player in the long term care insurance profession. He has mentored and trained thousands of agents on the art of building a successful practice as a LTC solutions specialist

Matt McCann

Director of Business Development at ACSIA Long Term Care

Phone: 630-698-0916

Email: mmccann@ltcglobal.com

Website: www.ltcopportunity.com

A former LTC insurance top producer, Matt has developed selling techniques and sales strategies that have been adopted by ACSIA nationally.

Chapter 41

What Is The Agent's Role When Clients Go On Claim?

By Margie Barrie

Q. *I have several clients who will soon need home health care. What advice can I provide to them and their families when they go on claim?*

Unfortunately, I just had personal experience with a home health care claim for my mother, a widow then age 90. To complicate the situation, I live 1000 miles away from my hometown, where my mother still resides in a very nice condo.

When my brother – who lives 75 minutes from her – took her to the hospital, she was diagnosed with double viral pneumonia and admitted. She was treated with an antibiotic that resulted in her becoming paralyzed in the groin. Five days later, her doctor told her that she had recovered enough so that Medicare would not pay for the hospital; she had to leave the next day. Meanwhile, she was still very weak.

She then went to a nursing home to learn how to walk again and eventually returned home with around-the-clock home health care. As she improved at home, we were able to cut back the care to seven hours a day – we convinced her to use a medical alert device when the aide was not on duty. Here was a woman who, before this occurred, walked a mile every day; now she is dependent on a walker and sometimes a wheelchair.

Here are the lessons I learned from this extremely traumatic experience:

1. Obviously there was total panic on her part: Where she would go? Who would take care of her? etc. I reassured her that it was not only her decision and not to stress. She had three people who would manage this situation – me, my brother and his wife (who is a doctor). And we could hire a care coordinator if needed.

Make sure your clients are aware of the value of a care coordinator. They should not be pressured by busy doctors, hospital social workers and nursing home personnel to make a snap decision.

2. Since my husband was her LTCI agent, I knew the name of the carrier and the telephone number. I didn't know her daily benefit or policy number.

Contact your clients and ask them who should have a copy of their policy's schedule page (children, siblings, attorney). You can also use this opportunity to get referrals and develop prospects and centers of influence.

3. I always advise agents to stay out of the claim. I followed my own advice and that definitely worked.

Help the family contact the claims department and let them take care of the claim, not you.

4. My sister-in-law Nancy made the initial arrangements with the agency to send a companion. My question was - is a companion actually a Certified Nursing Assistant, which her policy required? (Answer – yes.) My mom needed around-the-clock care – so the agency scheduled two 12 hour shifts. The daily cost was $440 – which seemed staggering at first until I realized it was about $18 an hour. And Nancy asked if the night shift person was supposed to stay awake or was she allowed to sleep. (Answer – she will do whatever the family wants.)

Let the carrier's claims department make sure that the HHC agency and the aide qualify for payment and that you know the type of care the agency is providing.

5. The carrier's intake specialist asked if my mother had a Financial Power of Attorney (and to fax it.) I didn't know, and it wasn't a good time to ask my mother.

Suggest to your clients that they obtain a Financial Power of Attorney and then give a copy to their children.

6. Being a long distance caregiver is tough. The guilt, lack of control, etc., are mind boggling. I'm still working on that. I do have peace of mind that my mom has a policy, the

claims department is working with the family and my mother is getting the care she needs.

Margie Barrie, LTCP

Author, columnist, LTC specialist
Phone: 941-355-7600
Email: info@margiebarrie.com
Website: margiebarrie.com
Margie is a LTCI expert who has written this book based on her experiences as an agent, the LTC columnist for *Senior Market Advisor* Magazine, the National Marketing Coordinator and master trainer for the LTCP Designation, the national vice president of the 3in4 Need More Campaign and the co-founder of Hagelman Barrie Sales Training Solutions.

Chapter 42

The Ten Commandments For Better Policy Placement

By Mark Goldberg & Margie Barrie

Q. *I want to increase my LTCI sales income this year by improving my placement rate. How can I accomplish that?*

To help you increase your placement rate – and have more policies stay on the books – here are our Ten Comandments for better policy placement. (The Commandments were created by Mark from the feedback of many of the profession's most prolific producers. Margie has added her own proven sales suggestions (in italics)).

I. Thou shall pre-qualify prospects for health and wealth at the time you set an appointment -

I use this script: "There are a lot of people in your age group who are looking into this protection, but a many of them can't qualify due to their health. So I need to ask you a few health questions to see if this is even relevant for you.

- In the last ten years, have you had any hospitalizations? When? What for?

- Any surgeries in the last five years?

- Any physical therapy in the last year?

- What prescriptions are you taking? Has the dosage been stable?

- Have you ever suffered a stroke, a heart attack, any type of cancer, hypertension disease or diabetes? (If diabetes, how do you treat it - insulin? How many mg? Oral medications? What is your current A1C Score?)

- Do you get around ok? Or do you have any need for a walker or cane?

- Is there anything else I need to know about your health?"

II. Thou shall use the carrier underwriting guides or underwriting hot lines for questionable health cases -

There are software programs like My LTC Office through LTC Connection that have loaded all the different criteria from the carriers into a program where if you just type in the condition they will display how each carrier will look at it when they underwrite the case. Also, I have a folder with the email addresses and toll-free numbers for all carrier underwriting departments. If I have any questions at all, I contact them.

III. Thou shall be a field interviewer and an active listener - I ask the clients to talk about their personal experiences and the consequences on the family and finances. It is important to receive agreement that clients think LTCI is the best solution for addressing their risks. They should be able to articulate why this is so.

I try to follow the 70/30 rule - 30% of the time I should be talking, and 70% the clients should be talking. Here are some good questions to use to start the conversation flowing:

- Have you or anyone you know had any experience with Home Care? Nursing Home Care? Assisted Living?

- How would LTC planning have changed your family's experience?

- Please share with me about your family, Children? Grandchildren? Where do they live?

- If you ever needed care, would you prefer to stay here in your home or move closer to where your family is located?

- Do you have a will? Did you designate the nursing home or hospital as a beneficiary in that will, because for many of us that is where much of our life savings can end up going as we get older?

IV. Thou shall qualify clients for health in more detail during the presentation - Have the carrier hot line number available to call or software to access on the spot if you learn more about health issues not evident before the interview. Ask clients with chronic conditions to explain the possible negative changes as a result of their condition, i.e., diabetes, high blood pressure, etc.

If during the appointment, I think there could be an underwriting problem or if I feel that the client may be withholding health information, say the following: "You need to tell me everything I need to know about your health history for the last five years. If there is something there, the insurance company will find out. So please let me know up front to avoid any surprises."

V. Thou shall take the time to learn about the prospect's finances - in order to properly design a plan that they will think delivers good value and won't cause sticker shock. Ask questions to understand their use of interest on investments and their cash flow. Seek to understand how it may change as time evolves, especially if they are not presently retired. A good general philosophy is to keep their premium at no more than one percent of their total liquid assets. Consider coinsuring the risk for wealthy clients and those with a dependable income regardless of where they're living.

If someone is hesitant to share this information, let them know you understand; and explain further that as an interviewer, it's your job to make a report based on both health and finances to the carrier. It also helps you when working with them to properly design and recommend a plan to meet their specific needs. You could use a question like: *"The average yearly cost of a nursing home is close to $80,000. Do you think you could cover the cost of care for at least one year without having to sell your home?"*

Then continue with some specific questions like: *"By the way, this is a very nice home. If you were to sell it, do you know what it may be worth in today's market? (Wait for the answer.) Do you own any other real estate? If yes, ask:What would you say the value of that is? Putting real estateaside, how much would you say you have approximately in savings and investments?"*

When you ask specifics about their finances, instead of general questions like how much money do you have, they are much more likely to cooperate.

There are two times during the sales process when I discuss finances.

1. When calling to set the appointment - *If I'm using direct mail leads that are based on the state Partnership program, I say "According to the state of _____, they recommend that you have at least $30,000 in assets excluding your home. Actually, I recommend at least $100,000. Do you fit into that group?"*

2. During the client interview when discussing the appropriate combination of benefits - *Then I probe a little deeper because I want to get a big picture of their finances. I want to make sure that they are not over-insuring and that the policy and benefits they select are appropriate.*

If you have a prospect with high assets, then they can get away with less insurance by co-insuring. And they will still benefit from having peace of mind that they have care coordination and aren't paying all of the bills on their own. Explain to them that since they have substantial assets, then the partnership may not come into play. However, things happen. People who have wealth today may not have it in years to come.

VI. Thou shall establish the reasons why clients should designate you as the professional to solve their LTCI needs - Once clients decide that LTCI is the proper solution for them to address their risk, they still need to determine you're the one with whom they should do business. Earn their respect as a professional who knows the products and can be trusted to offer recommendations that are in their best interest.

When working with clients via the internet, I include in my meeting confirmation e-mail my bio and a personal story about why I believe in LTC protection. If meeting face-to-face, I take a folder containing that information. Also, during the presentation, I emphasize that I am there to help them today and down the road when they need to access policy benefits.

VII. Honor thy clients by involving them in their plan design - Thou shall design a program and recommend a carrier for your prospects' specific needs and preferences for care. Take into account their finances, so they agree that LTCI is affordable and makes good financial sense.

Remember to acknowledge their desires for where they want to obtain care, at home, in a facility or even in another state. Be willing to guide your clients toward practical solutions. For example, single prospects may say they want to get all of their care at home. However, unless they can identify a reliable caregiving support system, they are much more likely to require a facility. In that case, you should advise them to protect themselves against the greater cost of a facility.

I am now using a technique that works incredibly well.

Step 1 – *I explain the four benefit choices that impact the premium - daily or monthly benefit amount, the benefit length, elimination period and inflation protection benefit.*

Step 2 – *I then provide guidelines for selecting the benefits that are most appropriate for them.*

Step 3 – *I guide them in selecting their initial combination of benefits. I explain that the richer the benefit the higher the premium, and the lower the benefit, the lower the premium. I emphasize that this is just a starting point so that we determine the initial premium amount. We can modify it based on their budget and/or comfort level.*

Step 4 – *I open my StrateCision software. I start with the carrier that will be my first choice for them. As they watch, I enter their names, ages, needed information and benefits selected. For the premium show the monthly amount.*

Step 5 - *Working together, we adjust the combination of benefits so that they are comfortable with the premium amount.*

Step 6 - *I show other carriers so we can shop together. I want them to understand that I represent all the top carriers in the industry and my goal is to do what is best for them.*

Step 7 - *I ask for the application*

VIII. Thou shall spend meaningful time with each client after the application and paperwork have been completed - Take the time to address questions or concerns. Ask again why the client is committed to needing a LTC policy. Consider outside factors, including input from children, financial advisors, friends and other advisors. If there are health issues, discuss what would happen if one of the applicants is declined. Make certain they understand the underwriting process and time line. Explain the next steps including phone interview, face-to-face assessment, doctor's records and their options at time of delivery.

IX. Thou shall honor thy client by allowing them to provide referrals - If you have done your job properly during the interview process, you should have moved from the role of salesperson to advocate. Clients should see you as an advisor who assisted with the design and approval of their policy. As a result, if they truly see the value of what you have done for them, they may want to let others know about your services. Giving clients the opportunity to share referrals with you shows that they appreciate your service. Healthy people tend to know other healthy people of the same socio-economic background. A strong recommendation will lead to more sales and higher placement rates.

X. Thou shall send clients a handwritten personal thank you note on the same day you take their applications - It's very important they hear from you immediately following your meeting. After clients make an application, they may experience negative thoughts such as, "Should we be doing this now?" or "Can we really afford it?" Hearing from you helps assures them that they made the right decision, and you were the right person to assist them.

I haven't done this as promptly as I should. I do send a thank you, but it is when I get to it. Mark, you are right. I now plan to start sending the thank you as soon as I return to my office.

And a Bonus Commandment . . . XI. Thou shall set an appointment to deliver the policy, preferably in person - Or set a time for a phone call for the day they receive the policy to review their coverage, especially the schedule page and exclusions sections. Confirm they feel comfortable with their policy design, premium, payment mode and the overall strategy of using LTCI to address this risk. It's important that you get them to express the emotional reason of why they took this important protection and that they are happy with the service and advice you provided. The time of delivery is another great opportunity to get referrals or start other conversations about other helpful products.

I have developed a whole process for delivering the policy whether in person or mailing it and explaining it over the internet. The process includes a written agenda with the client(s) name at the top. I have also developed a script that I use for asking for referrals both now and in the future.

Mark Goldberg
LTC Solutions Specialist
Email: mgoldb3181@aol.com
Starting as a producer in 1991, Mark has become a prominent player in the LTC insurance profession. He has mentored and trained thousands of agents on the art of building a successful practice as a LTC solutions specialist.

Margie Barrie, LTCP
Author, columnist, LTC Specialist
Phone: 941-355-7600
Email: info@margiebarrie.com
Website: margiebarrie.com
Margie is an LTCI expert who has written this book based on her experiences as an agent, the LTC columnist for *Senior Market Advisor* magazine, the National Marketing Coordinator and master trainer for the LTCP Designation, the national vice president of the 3in4 Need More Campaign and the co-founder of Hagelman Barrie Sales Training Solutions.

Chapter 43

Strategic Selling: Analyzing Your Audience To Better Target Your Message

By Jeremy Pincus

Q. *I want to analyze my clients from a market segmentation approach so I can determine what specific messages worked for the various types of people I have sold to. Then I will use this information to approach prospects. Has any research been done on this for selling LTC insurance?*

Note from Margie – Jeremy Pincus is well known in the LTC industry for this type of market research. I know you will find his contribution to this book very helpful.

Perhaps the most important consideration when attempting to market LTC insurance is the psychological motivation of your target audience. Consider Julie and Jack. Julie is a young single lawyer living in Manhattan, while Jack is a middle-aged electrical engineer in Omaha who has added an in-law apartment to his home. They are both extremely motivated to buy LTC insurance, yet they think of LTC issues in radically different ways. Because of the different ways they imagine their future LTC scenario, they will look for drastically different features and respond to wholly different stories, images and information.

Using interviews with nearly 4,000 American adults, my team and I used a variety of statistical techniques to segment the population according to distinct, categorical differences in their motivation to plan for a future LTC situation. What we discovered is that there are two main dimensions upon which people differ.

First, some people are planners by nature. They have an instinctive sense of responsibility and natural motivation to plan. For others, non-planners, this does not come naturally.

Second, some people are, by nature or circumstance, self-oriented. Their own personal safety and comfort are their primary concerns, as opposed to those who are family-oriented, think more collectively and are, for example, experienced at making personal sacrifices for the good of their family.

By crossing these primary sources of motivation, the market for LTC insurance should be considered in four broad segments:

- Family-oriented planners

- Family-oriented non-planners
- Self-oriented planners
- Self-oriented non-planners

These four groups of people exist in all adult life-stages (e.g., early adulthood, middle age/pre-retirement, retirement) but in different proportions. Nevertheless, each type represents a sizeable population. And because all of these types are prevalent among Americans with above average income, they are all potential prospects for LTC insurance.

The four segment types exist within each of the three age bands studied, younger Baby Boomers, older Baby Boomers and Eisenhower/GI generation, resulting in 12 distinct segments. These 12 segments vary dramatically with regard to LTCI ownership rates, purchase interest among non-owners, price sensitivity, responsiveness to specific plan features, resonance to product positioning and emotions, and channel usage and preferences.

Identifying the market segments

So, how can you figure out into which segment a particular prospect falls? For that matter, how can you tell which of the four segments predominates in a particular group of employees or within a particular association or other affinity group?

Fortunately, through the use of some sophisticated statistical modeling, we have identified a short series of key questions that pinpoint the interests and values of consumers that can be asked in person (one-on-one) or in group settings as part of a presentation. These key questions classify prospects based on any possible set of responses to the questions.

Alternatively, if you are involved with database marketing (i.e., direct mail or email marketing via lists), we have also created algorithms that can actually pre-identify segment membership so that you can fit the right message to the right prospect, or even pre-determine if a particular group is a good fit for your particular marketing mix.

The best approach to identifying types in person is to break down the task into the two dimensions that form the segments:

First, look for indicators of "planfulness." Does the prospect or group tend toward technical, analytical professions? There's a pretty strong tendency for actuaries, engineers, analysts, mathematicians and the like to be Planners. On the other hand, creative types who flourish in the arts, advertising, design, entertainment and publishing tend to shy away from planning for distant events. Another indicator might be where the prospect or group lives and works. Planners are more prevalent in conservative regions and neighborhoods (think Des Moines, Iowa), whereas Non-planners can be found more easily in trend-setting places such as Greenwich Village, San Francisco, Seattle, Austin, etc.

Next, look for personal characteristics that suggest a Self- or Family-orientation. Does the prospect or group live in a region of the country with a high or low divorce rate? For example, the divorce rate in Nevada is more than three times higher than the divorce rate in Massachusetts. This is only one indicator, but the myriad social factors that drive this finding make it such that Family-orientation is more prevalent in the Northeast and Self-orientation is more prevalent in the Southwest.

Of course, these are broad generalizations and there is no substitute for actually talking to prospects and asking them certain questions. Asking these questions properly depends upon engaging the customer in directed conversation. Whether selling group, multi-life, individual or association, occasions occur dealing with individuals one-on-one or with couples, whether in-person or on the phone. In these cases it is important to quickly identify segment membership in order to enact an effective marketing approach.

Prospects understand that, in order to provide proper information about the most relevant products, the salesperson will ask questions; similarly, websites ask "intake questions" in order to provide the most relevant content. Questions about one's home, family, employment and general lifestyle provide useful information and a low-pressure way to begin conversation. Once discussion becomes only a bit more personal, estimating a customer's segment becomes a matter of putting together their answers to a brief set of questions.

Strategic selling depends upon identifying the proper segment characterizing a prospective buyer. By distinguishing segment membership early in the process, it is possible to anticipate potential barriers to sales and identify potential solutions.

Selling to the segments

Understanding the four types of LTC insurance prospects is very useful for marketing purposes because the differences in motivation that underlie the segments translate to clear differences in a variety of marketing mix factors including:

- Their hot button issues

- The messages that will resonate

- The plan features that best address their psychological needs

- The premiums they are willing to pay

- The sales environment within which they will best respond

The consumer segment with the highest involvement among prospective buyers of LTC insurance is Self-oriented Planners. This is because this segment's interest in LTC insurance is driven by the perception that they personally will need care. In contrast, Family-oriented Planners strive for as much mastery over their lives as self-oriented planners, but are more driven by family values. Further, Family-oriented Non-Planners are fear-driven and overwhelmed by the responsibility of planning. The least involved of all are Self-oriented Non-Planners: unmotivated free spirits for whom planning is not so much an overwhelming challenge as a largely invisible non-priority.

Selling to family-oriented planners - This segment is motivated to protect their families from the burden of LTC and to simultaneously preserve assets for future use by their family. They feel personally responsible for engaging in and completing the necessary planning to avert a future crisis. Their interest in LTC planning tends to have been triggered by a family LTC situation. Emotionally, this segment is guilt-driven.

- Goal: Protect family, avoid burdening

- Message: Analytical approach (risk statistics, cost of LTC, cost of waiting)

- Plan Design: Core product, shared care, spousal discount

Selling to family-oriented non-planners - This segment believes that "family should take care of their own," rather than paying others to do it for them, which they view as a selfish dereliction of duty. This view extends to fear and hostility toward paid caregivers as strangers in the home. This group is also fearful of nursing homes and would "rather die" than live in one. Because of their belief in family-provided home-based care, this group tends to take a passive approach to LTC planning. Emotionally, this segment is fear-driven.

- Goal: Helps family care for you at home

- Message: Value, value, value

- Plan Design: Focus on maintaining family involvement with informal care benefits at lowest possible cost

Selling to self-oriented planners - This group tends to be single, divorced, separated or widowed, and, consequently, is concerned with how they can ensure that any future period of disability that befalls them is as comfortable as possible. They are already aware of the risk, so they don't need to be convinced. They need to see that their plan is as comprehensive, well-designed and flexible as possible. Because they look for quality above all, they are not price sensitive. Emotionally, this segment is control-driven.

- Goal: Control and comfort

- Message: Spreadsheet price/features, LTCi vs. investing

- Plan Design: Promote compounding inflation, cash benefits, choice of caregiver

Selling to self-oriented non-planners - This segment is unconcerned with burdening their family or even their own future well-being. Because their credo is to "live for today," the very concept of a future self that is disabled is unacceptable to them. They devalue these future possible selves and are not motivated to part with today's income that can be spent on themselves, to protect these future "others." They tend to deny that they are aging as they find this similarly unacceptable. Because they tend to be disconnected from their families, they have minimal experience with LTC situations. Emotionally, this segment is denial-driven.

- Goal: Help preserve pleasurable lifestyle

- Message: "You'd be dumb not to buy this"; stories, not statistics

- Plan Design: Simplicity above all

The bottom line is that segment-based marketing is perhaps more important when it comes to marketing LTC insurance than virtually any other product because the fundamental nature of the problem-to-be-solved by the product varies dramatically among different segments. Look at your marketing approach with a critical eye and ask yourself the question to which of these segments, if any, is my approach aligned?

Jeremy Pincus
Principal, Forbes Consulting Group
Phone: 781-863-5000 x 122
Email: jpincus@forbesconsulting.com
Website: www.forbesconsulting.com/ltc
Jeremy is a fact-based researcher and chronicler of the LTC insurance marketplace highlighting group LTCI, baby boomer trends and the role of women in the LTCI sale.

PART 6

How The
3in4 Campaign
Can
Benefit You

Health Care Isn't Enough

3in4 have requested more info about LTCi

Chapter 44

What Is The 3in4 Need More Campaign?

By Jonas Roeser

Q. *I've been hearing about the 3in4 Need More Campaign. What is it?*

It is a national awareness campaign that supports the education of planning for one's long term care needs. Our mission is to educate Americans about the need to form a long term care plan and what products, services and options could be part of their plan. The key message is "Health Insurance Isn't Enough, 3in4 Need More." And who better to raise this awareness and communicate this message than agents, financial advisors and planners.

The campaign provides a proven approach to help professionals in the LTC space successfully explain to their clients and prospects the need for planning. Here are the key facts on which the 3in4 concept is based:

- 77% of Americans age 30 to 65 think they should know more about LTC insurance than they currently do.[1] That's more than 3in4 of Americans.

- 74% of consumers age 55 to 65 said they are concerned about needing some kind of long term care.[1] Again that's nearly 3 in 4 of us.

I created the campaign when working as the Chief Marketing Officer at LTC Financial Partners, LLC (LTCFP). It was a very successful communication piece with many of our affinity accounts and consumer outreach, but the concept of turning it into a national non-profit open to the LTC industry was actually the idea of Scott Williams from John Hancock. LTCFP executives liked the idea of supporting the industry on this scale, hence the non-profit was formed and trademarks for the 3in4 were turned over to the newly formed 3in4 Association. The next big jump forward for the 3in4 Association was when I explained the concept to Margie Barrie and Mark Goldberg, and they both decided to support the cause. Our first move as the 3in4 Executive team was forming an advisory board.

The campaign focuses on four objectives:

1. Spread the word among the public that "3in4 Need More" than health insurance.

2. Support Congressional efforts to provide additional incentives like tax deductions or credits to help people better afford long term care products.

3. Bring the LTC industry together to educate the public by joining the 3in4 Need More Campaign and using the logo and visuals to spread the word.

4. Educate the public on private programs and federal entitlement options.

To increase the visibility of the need for LTC planning, the 3in4 Association has initiated a number of major events to gain industry and media attention. Three of the most visible events that have been conducted took place in 2011 and 2012. These events were two national bus tours across America and our New York City Times Square Flash Mob. The three events featured our national spokesperson, Dr. Marion Somers. She is a well-known geriatric care coordinator, book author and speaker.

The bus tour in 2011 stopped in the top ten Dominic Market Areas (DMA's) to conduct TV, radio and print interviews about the cause. The 2011 tour resulted in more than 122 million impressions from the print, online and broadcast coverage, with an estimated media value of $2.8 million in eight weeks.

The 2012 bus tour was a 12-week trip and was even more successful. As a result of the carefully orchestrated campaign, the tour resulted in over 299 million impressions across television, print, online and radio, with an overall media value estimated at $6.3 million. To view the bus tour videos, visit www.youtube.com/3in4needmore.

The campaign has also sponsored two national contests. For the 2011 Caregiver Contest, caregivers were asked to submit their "care" story through the 3in4 web site. The winner was featured in Dr. Marion's new TV pilot, *Dr. Marion to the Rescue.* To view a teaser of the pilot, go to www.drmariontotherescue.com. The winner received an in-home makeover for an elderly person (such as installing grab bars and ramps) and a "take care of the caregiver" makeover. The complete winner's package totaled approximately $50,000. The contest was announced at the launch of the tour live on *Fox N Friends* from New York City and received further exposure from both national and regional media outlets throughout the tour.

The 2012 tour featured a contest titled "Bring Your Talent" sponsored in conjunction with Emeritus Senior Living. As Dr. Marion traveled across the country with her bus and camera crew, they stopped at various Emeritus facilities to hold auditions. Talent performed either at Emeritus or on their own, and all the performances were uploaded to the contest Facebook page so the public could vote. The winner received a year's free rent at an Emeritus facility and 11 others won a week respite stay. Details can be seen at http://www.3in4needmore.com/dr-marion/senior-talent-contest/

Public relations events also included national press releases, radio public service announcements and 3in4 Need More commercials playing on CNN airport monitors.

To join the campaign, visit the website www.3in4needmore.com. Sign up and then review the information about how the campaign can support your business and drive national awareness about the need for LTC planning. Website information includes offerings for agents, agencies, vendors and strategic partners. To request additional information, email us at contact@3in4needmore.com.

Help us spread the word. Help the 3in4 campaign create even more public awareness of the need for LTC planning and invite others to join this incredibly important cause.

Jonas Roeser

President of Roeser Resources LLC
Phone: 206-245-4960
Email: Jonas@roeserresources.com
Website: www.roeserresources.com
Jonas is the founder and president of the 3in4 Association which operates the national LTC awareness campaign, 3in4 Need More. Roeser Resources is a full service branding and boutique marketing agency.

Footnotes
[1] Source - 2010 Prudential Long-Term Care Consumer Awareness & Attitudes Study

Chapter 45

How Can You Benefit From The 3in4 Campaign?

By Mark Goldberg & Jonas Roeser

Q. *How can I benefit from the 3in4 Campaign? When I visit the website, what can I receive by joining this effort?*

The campaign provides a number of ways for agents to be involved. It's free to join, and many of the materials are free as well. There are also other levels of membership that provide private labeled marketing materials, training and access to specialty branded lead generation campaigns through a third party vendor. When you join, details will be provided to you. Visit www.3in4NeedMore.com to review the offerings for agents, agencies, vendors and strategic partners.

Below is a list of free items one receives by joining:

- Powerpoint presentations and scripts to present at an association meeting such NAIFA or NAHU. They are both strategic partners of the 3in4 campaign.

- LTC resources list
- An article titled "12 Ways To Incorporate 3in4 Into Your Practice"
- 3in4 YouTube link
- Cost of Care Map for U.S.

The items below are available with the paid levels of membership.

- A listing as an LTC Resource on the www.3in4needmore.com. This enables a consumer to source a LTC specialist via their specialty by city and zip code.

Agent listings will also be present on our smart app, which will be released in 2013.

- 3in4 Booklet, "The Essentials of LTC Planning" – Ability to brand the book with one's bio, photo and contact information it is a valuable addition to any agents marketing efforts.
- Awareness materials that can be co-branded, contain agent contact information and image.
- Training on how to use the campaign and its tools to increase your marketing efforts.
- Access to third party 3in4 themed direct mail lead campaign.
- Greeting cards with the 3in4 theme

Visit www.3in4needmore.com to learn how the campaign can support your business. To request additional information email us at contact@3in4needmore.com.

Mark Goldberg
LTC Solutions Specialist
Email: mgoldb3181@aol.com
Starting as a producer in 1991 Mark has become a prominent player in the LTC insurance profession. He has mentored and trained thousands of agents on the art of building a successful practice as a LTC solutions specialist.

Jonas Roeser
President of Roeser Resources LLC
Phone: 206-245-4960
Email: Jonas@roeserresources.com
Website: www.roeserresources.com
Jonas is the founder and president of the 3in4 Association which operates the national LTC awareness campaign, 3in4 Need More. Roeser Resources is a full service branding and boutique marketing agency

Chapter 46

Using the 3in4 Need More Campaign To Drive Awareness And Support Sales

By Jonas C Roeser

Q. *How can I use the 3in4 Need More Campaign to support my sales and marketing efforts?*

Building awareness of need is the first step toward any buying decision. The 3in4 Need More Campaign starts conversations that opens minds and supports sales.

The 3in4 Need More logo and slogan drive home the need for LTC planning, gain attention, stimulate referrals and open doors to worksite/association educational meetings.

Here are three ways to use the 3in4 Need More Campaign to create opportunities.

1. Referrals from a consumer point of sale - Upon finishing writing the application, make the following statement to your new client/s. *"Mr. and Mrs. Jones, you did a wise thing taking out long term care insurance. I will keep you posted on your applications. Let's figure about six to eight weeks for a decision, and thank you again for your trust and business. As I support the guidance of your application through the underwriting process, I am requesting your support in a national LTC awareness campaign fueled by policy holders. Most Americans aren't insured for this kind of care and waiting to insure carries great risks. You took the steps today to start transferring your risk to an insurance carrier. Would you like to help your friends take these same steps? Since long term care will affect nearly 3 out of 4 people 65 or older, could you inform me of four names of people you would like me to provide the same education as I did for you today?"*

2. Using Facebook and the 3in4 Campaign together -

Step 1 - Search Facebook for your clients and send them a message requesting them to "Friend" you. (Did you know the fastest growing demographic on Facebook is women over the age of 55?)

Step 2 - Once your client has accepted you as their "Friend," send them the following message and request they post it on their Facebook "Wall" about their experience with you as a LTCI specialist. *"Friends and family, I purchased a long term care insurance plan from (insert agent's name here) to protect my assets and ensure that I will have the care needed if I should have a long term care experience. I highly recommend you take the time to meet with (insert agent name here); his/her contact info is* *below. Statistics show that nearly 3in4 people will need some kind of long term care. A long term care policy may not be right for you, but everybody needs a long term care plan. Do not wait until it is too late to buy a plan. This is one of the rare cases of a purchase where money is not the only factor for purchase; your health actually buys the plan, it's your money that funds it. Find out if a plan is appropriate for you by calling today. Help support the national campaign titled 3in4 Need More. To learn more about the campaign visit www.3in4needmore.com."*

3. Using the 3in4 Need More Campaign to align with a financial advisor - *"Mr./Ms. FA, I am calling to set an appointment so that I may provide you details regarding a possible risk exposure to many of your clients who you have under management. This exposure affects nearly 3 out of 4 clients. This meeting will take a total of 30 minutes and is critical. Could you imagine if close to 75 percent of your business started to stop investing with you, and 75 percent of the money under your management was subject to an average deduction of $219 per day? What day and time this week is best for you to continue our discussion?"*

If asked what the exposure is, follow up with: *"The exposure is not planning for your clients' long term care needs. As a financial advisor, you have helped your clients manage and grow their assets. Frequently clients are not aware of the rising cost of long term care, which in many cases can be the one area that can deplete their net worth very quickly. With the average private care rate being $219* *per day or $79,935 annually, could your clients afford to pay for this kind of care for multiple years? And even if they could, would they want to use their money accrued over all this time for such expenses?"*

"I am a specialist in plan design for long term care insurance. By spending an hour with each of your clients who are age appropriate, I can provide a plan that can cover these expenses. Why don't we start the process by you setting up four meetings where I will conduct an information exchange with your clients and provide a LTC plan? This way you can become comfortable with me as a specialist and see how I work first hand. How does this sound to you?"

More information on 3in4 Need More can be found at www.3in4needmore.com or by searching Google and YouTube.

———

Jonas Roeser
President of Roeser Resources LLC
Phone: 206-245-4960
Email: Jonas@roeserresources.com
Website: www.roeserresources.com
Jonas is the founder and president of the 3in4 Association which operates the national LTC awareness campaign, 3in4 Need More. Roeser Resources is a full service branding and boutique marketing agency.